Praise for *Go Slow to Grow Fast*

If you're a business owner or entrepreneur who's interested in growth, this book is a must-read. It's a practical case study for everyone who wants to grow a successful business.

—**Pat Cleary,** *President & CEO of National Association of Professional Employer Organizations*

Go Slow to Grow Fast *is an easy read that is well organized and practical. A great read for management teams experiencing or anticipating growth. I have several takeaways to share with my clients.*

—**Will Ditzler,** *Gazelles International Coach and Former CEO of mid-market growth firm*

This book defines what every business will experience no matter what product/ service or age of the organization. When broken down, Brent's insight is common sense, yet not common practice. With applicable takeaways and questions throughout the book, Go Slow to Grow Fast *will help you spend more time in the Driving Zone for your business.*

—**Aaron Prickel,** *President of Lushin Inc.*

Go Slow to Grow Fast *is an essential resource for CEOs and executive leadership teams of fast-growth firms. It helps them realize what it really takes to move through or avoid the dangerous Drama Zone. By understanding Brent's Quad 4 Model, the leadership teams I coach can discover better plans to address their blind spots and the disruptions that are sure to come.*

—**Dr. Craig Overmyer,** *Co-founder of Cultures That Work*
Gazelles International Certified Coach and Co-author of Success Is a Decision of the Mind

GO SLOW TO GROW FAST

GO SLOW TO GROW FAST

How to Keep Your Company
DRIVING AND THRIVING IN A FAST-PACED, COMPETITIVE BUSINESS WORLD

BRENT R. TILSON

ForbesBooks

Copyright © 2018 by Brent R. Tilson.

All rights reserved. No part of this book may be used or reproduced in any manner whatsoever without prior written consent of the author, except as provided by the United States of America copyright law.

Published by ForbesBooks, Charleston, South Carolina.
Member of Advantage Media Group.

ForbesBooks is a registered trademark, and the ForbesBooks colophon is a trademark of Forbes Media, LLC.

Printed in the United States of America.

10 9 8 7 6 5 4 3 2 1

ISBN: 978-1-946633-47-7
LCCN: 2018935205

Cover design by George Stevens.
Layout design by Megan Elger.

This publication is designed to provide accurate and authoritative information in regard to the subject matter covered. It is sold with the understanding that the publisher is not engaged in rendering legal, accounting, or other professional services. If legal advice or other expert assistance is required, the services of a competent professional person should be sought.

 Advantage Media Group is proud to be a part of the Tree Neutral® program. Tree Neutral offsets the number of trees consumed in the production and printing of this book by taking proactive steps such as planting trees in direct proportion to the number of trees used to print books. To learn more about Tree Neutral, please visit **www.treeneutral.com**.

Since 1917, the Forbes mission has remained constant. Global Champions of Entrepreneurial Capitalism. ForbesBooks exists to further that aim by bringing the Stories, Passion, and Knowledge of top thought leaders to the forefront. ForbesBooks brings you The Best in Business. To be considered for publication, please visit **www.forbesbooks.com**.

For my daughters, Becky, Brooke, Blair, and Brielle,
who inspire me to make the future better.

TABLE OF CONTENTS

FOREWORD

Successful executives exude magnetism, confidence, and vision. They motivate performance, command the respect of staff, and celebrate speed in building business. The 2017 Harvard Business Review article, "What Sets Successful CEOs Apart," surveyed the performance of 2,000 CEOs and identified decisiveness and impactful engagement as drivers of executive success. Effective business leaders consistently think steps ahead of everyone else in the organization. They inspire staff to act upon a dream of what the business can achieve.

The energy of its founder is enough to propel a small business forward. This is true because the organization is small, simple, and personable. A fast growth business, though, quickly becomes the victim of its own success. The organization grows in response to the charisma of the founder, but the energy of the founder becomes less and less efficient because the organization needs a refit to manage the complexity of larger size. An expanding mismatch between scale and organization can kill a good business. An MIT study found that one in four high-growth businesses fail within six years.

Through *Go Slow to Grow Fast*, Brent Tilson tells successful business leaders how to avoid this trap. Brent teaches executive leaders to leverage two other drivers of executive success identified in the Harvard Business Review article—proactive adaptation and reliable delivery of value.

A business founder's intuition about product and customer is often the seed of sales growth. Passion and "gut feel" enable more sales, but they can leave a business leader blind to the organizational stress of growth. A good management team communicates the cost of this stress, but a chief executive can myopically dismiss such concerns in favor of the emotional high of continued sales expansion. *Go Slow to Grow Fast* instructs business leaders to break this cycle, listen to their managers, and use a dashboard of indicators to make decisions that balance impact on scale and organization.

Readers learn through the story of Frank and Susan. Frank is the optimistic and hard-driving founder of a successful fast-growth business. He asks a consultant to meet with him and the firm's talented controller Susan to "fix morale." In contrast to Frank's rosy view of the business, Susan presents a stark picture of stress embodied by lower productivity, higher turnover, and deficient customer support. Frank learns that "low morale" is really a symptom of unsustainable business practice. Lack of planning for revenue growth has generated a disproportional increase in expenses. Frank and Susan rally around a new decision dashboard that insures balance in growth between sales and organizational capacity.

The story of Frank and Susan generates practical lessons for leaders. Return on investment (ROI) and revenue per employee (RPE) are the key business indicators. A rising ROI but a falling RPE signals unsustainable growth that takes a company into the "Drama Zone." Implementation of the right dashboard can return a company to the "Driving Zone" where both ROI and RPE are increasing. The journey from Drama Zone to Driving Zone is described by the author's "Quad 4 Model" which explains four predictable stages of business evolution.

In this quick read, business leaders learn to avoid a predictable blind spot when growing. The Quad 4 Model efficiently communicates insights derived from microeconomics and taught in business school. Clarity of insight comes from Brent Tilson's experience as a nationally accomplished entrepreneur, consultant, and civic leader. Genius is the ability to crystallize complicated concepts into simple action. *Go Slow to Grow Fast* delivers this in spades. The better executive decisions enabled by Brent's message embody the mission of his alma mater, the highly ranked Indiana University Kelley School of Business.

As a faculty member and associate dean within the Kelley School, I proudly offer these words as testament of the business wisdom each reader will receive and can immediately apply.

Professor Philip T. Powell
Associate Dean of Academic Programs, Daniel C. Smith Faculty Fellow
Indiana University Kelley School of Business
Bloomington & Indianapolis, Indiana

INTRODUCTION

Early in my entrepreneurial career as a CPA, I worked with a lot of small businesses and found that while all of them were facing different challenges and issues, there was a commonality among them that I couldn't yet explain. There was a cyclical nature to the issues, and I was trying to come up with a frame of reference to help guide and advise these businesses. Then I attended a continuing education program for CPAs, and the lecturer introduced a concept that intrigued me deeply. The S-curve life cycle of businesses that he presented that day explained simply the challenges that some of my clients were facing. That one-hour course sent me on a relentless pursuit of ways to help entrepreneurs navigate the complicated life cycles they would face.

My story began while I was in high school. I knew then that I wanted to be an entrepreneur, to follow in the footsteps of my great grandfather, a successful attorney. While he passed away many years before I was born, I was enamored in the family stories of his career.

With the entrepreneurial bug, I was quickly drawn into pursuing a degree in accounting, which would provide the foundational knowledge that I could use in my future and unknown career. This decision was transformational. I put all of my energy into pursuing an accounting degree and subsequently began my professional career with KPMG Peat Marwick, a Big Eight accounting firm at that time.

It wasn't long after I began my accounting career that I set my sights on opening my own firm. I knew I needed to learn as much as I could before venturing out on my own, but I soon realized that the large publicly traded and institutional businesses where I spent my time auditing and providing tax services wouldn't give me the unique experience and knowledge I'd get with working with entrepreneurial businesses.

After two years working in the Big Eight world, I was offered a position with the largest local firm, which specialized in entrepreneurial businesses, and I was hooked. I was fascinated with their clients' business models and challenges.

When I'd attained my required three years' experience and my CPA certification was under my belt, I decided it was time to pursue my first entrepreneurial business: my own CPA firm.

During those first few years, I got quick exposure to the challenges that entrepreneurs face, including myself. I engrossed myself with my clients, helping them with their business plans and strategies. It was during this time that I began my relentless pursuit of ways to help them navigate the S-curve life cycles they would encounter.

It didn't take long for me to realize that many entrepreneurs can't focus on their core business and skills while at the same time being pulled in many directions merely to run their business. Just hiring their first employee places ongoing pressures and demands that take them away from running their business. So, three years after starting my CPA firm, I started a new business to free them from this burden.

In 1995, I started a professional employer organization (PEO) to provide businesses with resources to help them focus on the business of their business while my firm manages the complicated details related to employees and HR. Working with entrepreneurial businesses over the years, I have been able to provide them with resources that have enabled them to grow and thrive.

The entrepreneurial community responded, as my new company was recognized as one of the fastest growing companies in the nation in 2001, 2002, and 2003 by *Inc.*. More notably, my company doubled in size between 2015 and 2016. I was not only helping businesses succeed, but also feeling the pressures myself. I was living the S-curve life cycle and continuously pursuing the solution to align growth and operational ability.

This book is a culmination of my years of working with entrepreneurs and the organizational issues they face as they try to balance financial and operational success. Along the way, I developed the Quad 4 business model to provide entrepreneurs the guidance to create high-performance businesses that align both finance and operations.

As you read this book, I will take you on a path of self-discovery, using a fable drawn from my many years of working with entrepreneurs much like you. I imagine that you will know both a "Frank" and a "Susan" in your own life, and maybe in some ways they might be you. My motto is "Go Slow to Grow Fast," and I hope this book offers the opportunity for business leaders to step back from their day-to-day work, look at the big picture, and learn to grow effectively.

CHAPTER 1

Losing Traction

The email read:

> *Subject: Need help with employee morale*
>
> *Brent, I recently heard you speak at a conference about building a high-performance business and could use some help with our employee morale. We have always had a Get It Done work ethic around here, but now we are having a culture clash between our seasoned and new employees. I think it is a by-product of our recent growth.*
>
> *Would you be available to meet with my controller, Susan, and me? We could use some help and guidance. Are you available next Monday at 2 p.m.?*

I look forward to hearing from you.

Regards,

Frank
President
Preferred Engineering

It was a brief email, but it spoke volumes to me. If my intuition was right, this was much more than a morale problem.

It was a classic Lifeline problem.

I replied and said I'd be happy to meet with them at that time. I requested that we meet in a room with a whiteboard or flip charts, and asked that he and Susan each complete an HR questionnaire that I sent along, on their own and not comparing answers, and bring it to the meeting.

To prepare for the meeting, I did some online research, and a recent story about Frank and his company in a community magazine caught my eye. It was titled "Local Entrepreneur Engineers Success." I learned that Frank started his engineering firm fifteen years ago and that today they were enjoying phenomenal success. The company had grown from thirty-five to eighty employees over the past three years. They'd landed some large new contracts with multi-state clients that had helped propel the growth. In addition, Frank was excited that he had been able to hire some highly experienced professionals to join his company and support its growth. I also learned that Frank had graduated from a prestigious university with a bachelor's degree in engineering, and that Susan and a few other employees had been with the company from the beginning. Frank had built a reputable business and was praised for its growth and success by other local businesses quoted in the article.

THE MEETING

I arrived for our meeting ten minutes ahead of our scheduled time and went to the front desk, where I was met with a note: "Please call extension 107." I did as instructed, and the voice on the other end answered, "This is Amanda," in a slightly irritated tone. I informed Amanda that I was in the lobby and had a 2 p.m. appointment with Frank and Susan. Amanda asked me to take a seat and said she would let them know I was in the lobby.

It was about 2:10 p.m. when Susan came and took me to the conference room. My initial reaction was that the conference room was heavily used. The conference table was large enough for ten people and also had three large whiteboards filled with information about sales, Gantt charts, and projects. I took my seat at the first chair next to the head of the table. Susan sat directly across from me, and then Frank joined us and sat at the head. They both brought their completed HR questionnaires.

Susan waved her questionnaire. "This was tough for me to complete," she said. "I do the HR for the company and I felt a little bit like we're failing in many of the areas."

Frank jumped in. "I did the best I could, but Susan really has a better handle on many of the areas in the questionnaire. I noticed it didn't ask much about morale, but I guess we'll get to that."

After sharing pleasantries, I asked, "Can you tell me about what instigated your email to me?"

Frank started first. "I attended a recent Chamber meeting where you gave a presentation on building high-performance businesses, and the part about morale really got me thinking. As I said in my email, we have a Get It Done work ethic around here, and now with all of our new employees and growth we're having a culture clash between seasoned and newer employees. This is also having an impact on our client relationships. Last week was the last straw. One of my oldest clients called to let me know that he didn't like the attitude and rudeness of one of our new engineers, Bill, and that if we didn't make a change he might look elsewhere for his engineering services. Also, Bill had been making mistakes that the client hadn't seen with prior employees. I knew at that moment that we had to take this seriously. Bill is a very talented engineer and this came as a surprise, because he's normally very easy to work with."

Susan chimed in. "Bill is easy to work with, but he's also working on many projects right now and putting in long hours. In fact, with all of our growth over the past couple of years, we're all putting in long hours."

My initial reaction to the email was correct—this was going to be a lot bigger project than just conducting a morale assessment and improvement initiative. The clues I was beginning to uncover told me we needed to gather a lot more data before we could begin solving the problem. In other words, we first needed to Go Slow, and find the root cause and issues. My suspicion was that it wasn't going to be easy.

"Before we get to discussing the company's morale, can you tell me about your company's history?" I asked. "You know, the basics— your personal background, why did you get into business, personal goals, successes, challenges, plans for the future?"

Frank seemed hesitant to share such details, but after a short pause he said, "I started my career working for a large engineering firm here in town. It was a great place to start out, as I was able to work on some large projects, they had a nice training program that helped me learn how to apply what I learned in college in the real world, and I was exposed to many facets of the business, from proposals to managing projects to hitting budgets. After about five years, I became restless—I got the entrepreneurial bug and wanted to start my own engineering firm.

"With a small loan, new business cards, and fear of failure, I started this company fifteen years ago. My goal was to replace my prior salary as fast as possible, so I'd make sales calls during the day and work on my projects in the evening. It was a very challenging time, as I was married with two young daughters at home, and I was trying to keep a balance between making money and spending time with my family. I quickly learned that I needed help in the office to keep the company moving. Susan was one of my first hires. I needed help with the paperwork, you know, accounting, taxes, all the headaches."

Susan chimed in, "Yes, and it was the smartest thing he ever did."

Frank was now fully engaged and seemed to enjoy reminiscing about the history of the company. "After about three years, we started having some solid success. We landed contracts with some larger clients that provided us steady work. My clients liked the fact that they could talk and work directly with the owner of the firm, and I was able to be super responsive to their needs. By this time, we had around ten employees."

I interrupted, "Frank or maybe Susan, do you recall what your gross revenues were at that time?"

Frank laughed and said, "That's Susan's job."

"It was probably around $1.5 million," Susan said. "I can look it up pretty quickly if you want."

"No, that's OK, we can dig into that later," I said. "Yet, let me ask a few more questions before we continue. I know it has been a long time, but do you recall how you were driving the revenue? Were the contracts at high hourly bill rates, or were you having to work long hours to generate the revenue?"

Frank responded quickly, "I remember very well. We worked long hours. It was very common for us to work sixty to seventy hours a week back then. We were lean and mean."

"That's hard to sustain," I said. "Did you have any employee turnover during that time?"

"Yes, unfortunately, one of my best engineers left in the middle of a big project."

"Did that have a negative impact on the company or other employees?" I asked.

"Actually, it did," Frank said. "It was a very busy time for the company, and when Damon left we were understaffed and unable to meet a few of our commitments. That was the beginning of a rough period for us. We lost the large client and had some other client challenges as well. But we worked through it, and it made us better in the end."

I wanted to push down on this comment. "So, Frank, what did you work through and what made you better?"

"At that time, each of the engineers managed their own projects and scheduling," he said, "and when Damon left we had a lot of trouble picking up the pieces to determine where we were in the project. We found that it was much further behind schedule than we realized, and in the end we lost that client. We couldn't let that happen again. As we looked at how we were managing projects, we realized we needed better systems to track them and better reporting so that we could resolve client issues more quickly. In fact, that was a major turning point for us as a company. We realized that if we didn't implement these new systems, we wouldn't be able to sustain growth and maintain the level of service our clients expected."

This was an impressive first five years of business for Frank. Few companies can grow to $1.5 million in revenue that quickly with only ten employees. I made a mental note that when he went through a rough spot, Frank recognized it and made some changes to his systems and processes in order to continue growing.

Frank continued, "After we got things turned around, our growth really took off. We grew about 20 to 30 percent each year. We had a few more rough spots over that time, but generally we were able to keep our clients and employees happy."

"Let's talk about the last twenty-four months," I said. "Your website mentions that you've added some major new contracts and more than doubled your staff. That's a major accomplishment. Tell me about how the company is doing."

"It has been thrilling," Frank said. "We've been pushing hard to break into larger national clients, and we were fortunate a couple years ago to land a major contract with a national company that has led to some other large contracts. This is what drove us to double the size of our staff. Not only have we hired a lot of new people, but we had to hire additional experienced engineering professionals to work on these larger accounts. Also, we had to hire more administrative staff and expand our support teams. It almost feels like we are a fifteen-year-old start-up. There's a lot of energy around the company. We have employees spanning the generations, and everyone is working hard to meet the needs of this exciting growth."

I was keeping an eye on Susan during Frank's explanation of the past two years, and she didn't have the same excitement and enthusiasm on her face as Frank. "If you don't mind, may I ask Susan the same question I asked you? She doesn't seem as enthused as you do."

Before I could ask Susan, she jumped at the opportunity to tell her side. "Frank has built a great company," she started. "It has been exciting to work with him from the beginning and to watch the company grow into what it has become today. Please keep in mind that my role is controller and human resources for the company, so my comments come from a different perspective. The growth is exciting, but it's expensive. Also, in hiring so many new employees, our culture has been changing. We seem to have lost our smaller company feel and the whole reason why many of the original staff loved working for Frank."

"Susan, can you expand on your comment about how growth is expensive?" I asked.

"Well, first I can see it on our financial statements," she said. "We've had to hire employees ahead of the revenue so that we can get them hired and trained, we've had to expand our office space and fill it with furniture, and our technology systems are being pushed to the limit. In fact, while our revenue is up substantially compared to two years ago, our profits for the last quarter are sharply down.

"The other challenge is the headaches that come from employee turnover," she continued. "We had to hire people so quickly that we hired some people we shouldn't have. I believe this is part of the reason for our morale problems. The original employees are being pulled in many directions to help train the new employees, and not all of the new employees seem to have the same work ethic. I could go on and on regarding employees—rumors, complaints, out-of-date policies. My to-do list gets longer every day."

Sensing the anxiety that had now filled the room, I decided it was time to help frame our conversation. I got up from my chair and approached the whiteboard. I turned and asked, "Are you familiar with the business S-curve life cycle?" Both Frank and Susan shook their heads and said no. "Over my years of working with and advising businesses, it has been helpful to get their gut reaction about where they'd plot their business performance on this simple chart," I said, as I reached for the board and drew a simple XY axis chart. I labeled the Y axis "Performance" and the X axis "Time." In the body of the chart I drew a curvy line from the bottom left to the top right.

Performance and Time

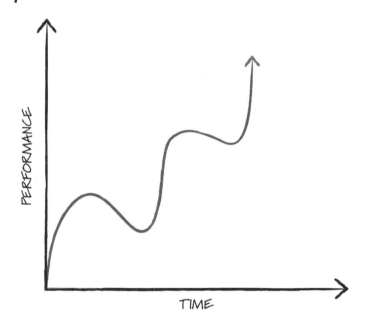

"Let me break it down simply," I said. "Over their lives, businesses all face similar issues related to performance over time. This curvy line represents that life cycle. Yet, it is much more than S-curves. At a deeper level, it represents the metaphorical life of a business. That is why I call it the 'Lifeline.' The portions of the line that are going up represent the company running smoothly and profitably—or 'Driving.' The portions of the line going down represent the company having problems and/or struggling—in other words, 'Drama.' The bottom of a trough represents that point where the company either makes improvements and begins the upward trend or faces negative consequences."

I made an "X" on the line just as it began down the first trough. "As an example," I said, "this would represent the point after three years when Damon left the company and you lost your large client. The bottom of this trough is when the new systems and processes were in place and you began to grow and perform well again. As you've gone through the years, these other troughs represent those periods when your business suffered through Drama and changes had to be made to get to the next level. My question to you is, where would you plot your company on this chart today?"

Frank stepped up to the whiteboard and made an X on the Lifeline. "Frank," I said, "we now have a frame of reference for the future and the decisions that will be made."

THE LIFELINE^{SM}

Where did Frank plot his company on the Lifeline? Where should he plot it? Would Susan and Frank agree on the location? Over the years, the conversations I've had with hundreds of business leaders have helped plan a course of action for smoothing out their Lifeline and the performance of their company in order to drive high-performing businesses.

> *The reality is that the path of a company's Lifeline is the direct result of management's decisions given the variables they face.*

The reality is that the path of a company's Lifeline is the direct result of management's decisions given the variables they face.

Ideally, a company's Lifeline would look much like the following graph. With this Lifeline, a company would have consistent growth in revenues and very little Drama. Although there is some fluctuation, the company has made decisions to anticipate change and prepare for the future.

Performance and Time

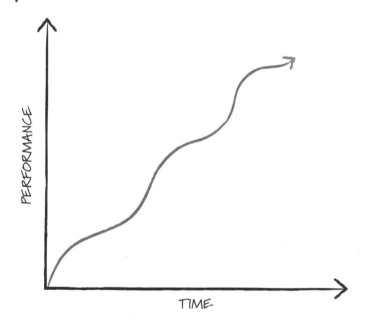

This is very difficult to do, and variables such as growth rate make it more difficult to have a smooth Lifeline. In fact, most companies would look more like this graph:

Performance and Time

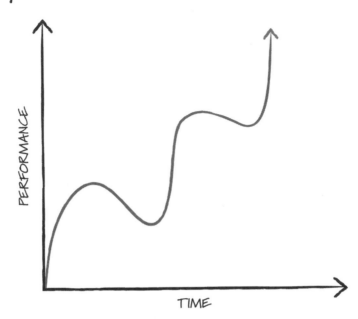

The goal is to provide management with the information they need to make decisions that keep the Lifeline as smooth as possible and the Drama period as short as possible. The reality is that businesses often outgrow their capability and experience negative consequences that can have modest to severe results.

Below are two comparative income statements. Both companies have similar revenues, expenses, and profits. From the information provided, which company will thrive and which company will experience Drama?

COMPARATIVE INCOME STATEMENTS			
Company A		Company B	
Revenue	$2,800,000	Revenue	$2,600,000
Expenses	$2,500,000	Expenses	$2,200,000
Net Income	$ 300,000	Net Income	$ 400,000

Obviously, we don't have enough information to know. Yet, this is often the only information that business leaders use to measure performance—they only look at their bottom line. Sadly, not only do business leaders use this as their primary measurement tool, but many stakeholders who support these leaders use the same information.

The reality is that we need to know much more information than just profitability. Profitability, while a measurement of business performance, often disguises business capability.

BUSINESS CAPABILITY

Ideally, management teams strive to align their business's capability with growth to maximize profitability. Yet over the long run, a company's profitability is a by-product of business capability.

> *Profitability, while a measurement of business performance, often disguises business capability.*

A business's capability is determined by decisions made by management over time on how to operate and manage the business. These decisions include everything from how and whom to hire, to which CPA firm to use, the location of the business, and the number of production cycles. A business's capability is truly the sum of all of management's decisions.

In Frank's story, his company had experienced successful growth in the early years and they were relying on brute force to run the company—employees working long hours to make sure the company generated revenues and the profits to survive. Yet the underlying organizational structure was fragile, and when Damon left the company, Frank quickly became aware of the underlying weaknesses in his systems and processes. This quickly led to a drop in revenue as they lost a major client. Frank smartly identified that his problem was not merely losing a key employee; it was also the fact that his existing systems couldn't support their current size and certainly wouldn't support them as they grew.

What we know from Frank is that his company didn't stop growing at this particular point. He added systems and processes to manage their projects and improve their client service. But what would have happened if Frank had not identified and made those important changes? Most likely, his business would have stalled, and over time it may have become another small business failure statistic.

> *According to a 2016 SBA report, approximately 50 percent of businesses fail in the first five years.*

FRANK MAKES HIS MARK

In Frank's case, he survived, as indicated by the number of Drama cycles that appeared on the chart between the one I marked where Damon left the company and where Frank marked his company today. Next, it was Susan's turn to make her mark on the company Lifeline. As she made her X, she turned to Frank and said, "I know this will upset you, but it is how it feels to me."

Key Takeaways

○ Every business has its own historical story and Lifeline. If you were to draw your Lifeline, what would it look like? Would it be smooth with slight valleys, or would it be volatile with highs and lows?

○ Draw your own Lifeline and indicate the major points along the line when you were in the Driving Zone and those when you were in the Drama Zone. Where are you today?

○ The faster your company is growing, the higher the operational risk. Did your Drama Zones occur soon after a period of high growth? If you are growing faster than 20 percent today, is your operational effectiveness keeping up with the growth?

○ The Lifeline is the accumulation of all of your management decisions over the history of your business. What are you using today to monitor the quality of your decision making?

As you continue this journey with Frank and Susan, it is my hope that from this point forward you will find nuggets of advice to implement in your business that will allow it to thrive in the Driving Zone.

CHAPTER 2

Slipping Out of Gear

I wasn't surprised by Susan's perspective. It was obvious from her comments that she was living in the Drama Zone. She was facing the daily challenges, and Frank seemed to be running his company by his gut intuition. It was time to introduce them both to the critical number. Now the Drama was about to increase.

Frank let out a frustrated laugh under his breath and said, "C'mon, it can't be that bad." Frank and Susan obviously had different views on where on the Lifeline the company was. Frank had marked his X on the Lifeline going up, but Susan had made her X two-thirds of the way down the curve heading towards the bottom and added an arrow pointing down to emphasize how she felt. Essentially, Frank and Susan viewed themselves at equal places opposite from each other.

Performance and Time

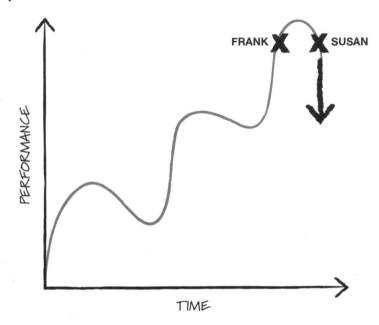

Susan responded defensively with an elevated voice, "Frank, we have a lot of Drama." I quickly jumped up from my seat and back to the whiteboard. I could feel that the tension in the room had some deeper history than just me asking them to indicate how they felt the company was doing. I made a mental note: maybe Susan was a part of the morale issue.

Susan made her way back to her seat, and I could see that she was visibly upset. Frank seemed irritated by the brief exchange, and, shaking his head, he turned to me and said, "I'm sorry. We've had some debates about the company lately and we seem to be on different pages."

"Maybe that's why I'm here," I responded.

Now I needed to understand why they had such different opinions. From my experience working with other entrepreneurs, I have found that many of them are eternal optimists. They like a good challenge and often get a thrill from running their businesses on the edge. Yet sometimes they look past signs of trouble, expecting that they will take care of themselves.

"At this point, this is how you feel about the business," I said, "but feelings are often rooted in your experiences. Let's talk about why both of you feel the way you do about the company. Frank, what led you to put your X where you did?"

"We've had so much success over the past couple of years, landing some large new clients that we've been pursuing for years," Frank said, pointing to the plaques on the wall with the logos of their prestigious clients. "We've added some really talented new employees, expanded the management team, and hired a new COO. While I admit we have a little Drama, I don't think it would put us in the Drama cycle. We are Driving," he added with passion and confidence.

I was a little confused, as this seemed in contrast to what he had said previously. "What about your comment earlier that you are having morale problems and it is having a negative impact on your clients?" I asked.

Frank responded quickly. "That's why I called you to help us with our morale. Everything has been going very well for the company, and once we get the morale fixed, everything will be great."

I turned to Susan. "Why do you think the company is deep in a Drama cycle?"

I noticed that the small spat between them had caused Susan to become slightly flushed. This was certainly an emotional conversation for her.

Susan took a deep breath and said, "I guess it's because of my role in the company. As the controller, I'm very aware of the pressures we're facing financially, and as the HR person, I am aware of the pressures we're facing with our employees. Everything seems to run through me. For example, Frank is right that we have large new clients with large contracts, but they are very bureaucratic and we don't get paid as quickly as with our smaller clients. Sometimes we don't get paid on our invoices for ninety days or more. And while it's great that we've expanded our management team, they are still learning their way around here, and it seems like I have one of them in my office every thirty minutes with either a question or an issue." Susan seemed exhausted as she shared her perspective.

It was all becoming very clear.

On the whiteboard, I drew vertical and horizontal crossing lines and started. "Let me try to frame our conversation. A young girl wants to learn how to ride a bike, and her dad agrees to teach her. So he puts training wheels on the bike and is there with her as she takes her first voyage. She eventually believes she's ready to take off the training wheels. But her dad knows that she doesn't know what she doesn't know about learning to ride. Psychologists refer to this as the Unconscious Incompetence stage. Her dad knows that she needs to learn to maintain both momentum and balance to ride, but she hasn't yet learned to put them together.

"After falling for the first time, she quickly learns that she doesn't know how to ride. Let's call this the Conscious Incompetence stage. As time goes on, with effort, she is highly focused on her peddling and balance, and she is so excited that she can ride her bike. We will call this the Conscious Competence stage. She learns that if she doesn't pay close attention to what she's doing, she will fall. One day, she hops on her bike and as she zips down the street to a friend's house, she doesn't even have to think about what she has to do to ride it. This stage is the Unconscious Competence stage." By now I had filled in each of the stages on the whiteboard.

Stages of Competence

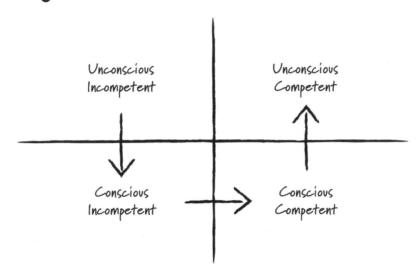

"This same analogy can be applied to driving a car. After years of driving, an experienced driver can monitor traffic, change lanes, adjust speed, shift gears, and avoid trouble while talking on the phone," I stated. "Isn't running a business much the same?

"A new entrepreneur doesn't know what they don't know, yet after years of experience they learn to run their business, much like an experienced driver. But what if that driver were put into the Indianapolis 500 and they were racing at speeds over two hundred miles an hour? What would happen? Probably just like the little girl learning to ride her bike, the driver would quickly wreck. The same holds true for business leaders. They learn to run their business and, as it grows at a controllable pace, they're able to learn and adjust to their changing environment. However, if the company grows too fast, the business leaders may struggle to manage their new reality and trouble begins.

"Thus their business's capability is similar to a driver's capability. The business must continually grow their capability or face the risk of a wreck. Not all wrecks are the same. Some are fender benders, but others end up in the salvage yard. My motto is 'Go Slow to Grow Fast.' The key is to Go Slow and truly understand the business's current capability, and then make any course corrections needed to Grow Fast without risking a wreck."

Frank nodded his head in agreement and said, "I agree with that analogy. Over the years, I've had to learn the hard way, and that's why I've expanded my management team and hired experienced professionals from large firms. I quickly recognized as we started growing that I needed to strengthen my team. Our original staff is outstanding, but many of them had never worked on larger accounts, and we were going to need to work on projects in teams instead of individually as we did historically." I was impressed with Frank's intuitiveness. It was obvious that he had thought through the needs of the business.

Frank felt like the company was going in the right direction, but Susan didn't agree. We needed to find out which view was right. "I know you asked me to come help you with morale, but first we need to come to an agreement on where you are on the Lifeline. Is the company in the Driving Zone or in the Drama Zone?" I asked.

I turned to Susan. "You mentioned that while your revenue has grown dramatically, your profits are down. Can you tell me what's driving the lower profitability?"

Susan responded, "Compensation is our largest expense, and it has grown dramatically over the past two years."

"How about on the revenue side? Have you had good client retention—any challenges in that area?"

"We've lost a few of our smaller clients," she responded, "and we've had to write off some of our billings due to mistakes to satisfy some others. But otherwise we seem to be doing fine."

"This is a question for both of you," I said. "Do you have a target revenue per employee, and if so, are you hitting your target?" Frank leaned back in his chair and looked toward the ceiling as he pondered the question. After a few seconds in silence, he said, "That's a great question. Susan, is that something you track? I know I don't."

Susan was also contemplating the question. "No, we measure billable time but not revenue per employee," she said.

"Let's go back to the analogy of the driver of the car. We know that the driver can monitor his speed by merely looking at the speedometer. But what else does he have on his dashboard? Gas gauge, tachometer, tire pressure light, and engine light, to name a few," I said. "While this may seem obvious, these all provide the driver with important information about how the car will perform. The driver may be going the speed limit, but if he's in the wrong gear the tachometer could be redlining."

Frank flashed a quick grin and jokingly said, "We're in the Driving Zone … we just need everyone to be in the right gear."

DRIVING AN EFFECTIVE BUSINESS

It was apparent that Frank and Susan did not agree on how the company was performing. Frank seemed to be measuring the success based on the overall growth of the company, the new larger clients, and hiring experienced professionals including a new COO. Susan, on the other hand, was measuring the success based on internal factors such as a declining bottom line, employee issues, and her overall frustration. Also, while we didn't discuss it, it is safe to assume that their cash flow had been impacted by the growth and mix of new business in addition to increased staffing. Most likely this added additional stress to Susan as the controller.

It is relatively easy to measure financial results or efficiency. Gross revenues, expenses, and profits are easily tracked and measured. In fact, companies monitor their sales on a daily, weekly, or monthly basis depending on their sales cycles. The data is readily available and monitored. But it is much more difficult to monitor a company's operational effectiveness. How does management know when their growth has achieved a level where their underlying systems are under stress in supporting the demands on the organization?

One of the easiest and best measures of organizational effective- ness, which is a broader and more general concept than operational effectiveness, is revenue per employee (RPE), measured simply by dividing the company's revenue by the current number of employees.

$$\frac{\text{Revenue}}{\text{Number of Employees}}$$

In an ideal world, a company would want to have the highest RPE possible, because that indicates high operational effectiveness. The reason RPE is the best measurement is that it measures how effectively a company is using all of its resources to generate revenue.

Revenue per employee is the ultimate critical number.

RPE is most useful when compared within the same industry. The software industry, for example, has a much different RPE than a law firm. This measurement provides leaders with the information they need to understand how they are competing in the marketplace compared to their competitors, and it is also important in monitoring effectiveness in a period of high growth.

Business growth is the one variable for businesses that has the largest impact on managing RPE. Companies with modest growth can more easily manage the timing of hiring, training, and getting employees to their full potential. However, fast-growing companies often outgrow their operational effectiveness and have to hire more people to support their growth.

To demonstrate this impact, a recent study found that, on average, Inc. 5000 companies generate 31 percent less revenue per employee than normal companies and employ 53 percent more employees.

Average Revenue Per Employee

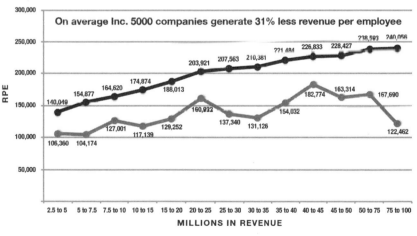

Forty.com—Inside the Inc. 5000: what it takes to be a high growth company—from the 2011 list

Average Employee Counts

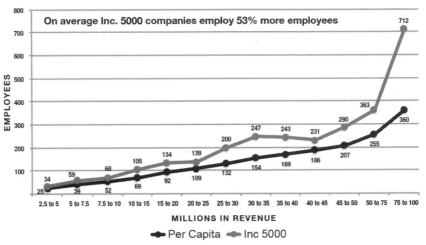

Forty.com—Inside the Inc. 5000: what it takes to be a high growth company—from the 2011 list

Beyond the obvious reason for the decrease in RPE in high-growth firms—namely, hiring employees before the revenue—there are other underlying issues that may arise that negatively impact operational effectiveness. First, the average tenure of employees will quickly drop as a result of employee growth. This will put significant pressure on training the new employees and bringing them to their full potential as quickly as possible. Next, turnover will most likely increase, as some tenured employees may not embrace the new and expanded operation. Almost unavoidably, some of the new hires will not meet the needs and will need to be replaced, further increasing turnover rates. Finally, company culture and morale will come under pressure from the changes within the company.

Frank's business was experiencing all of these issues and more, as he had grown at such a rapid pace and hadn't taken the necessary steps to Go Slow and prepare the organization to Grow Fast. He was managing the company the same as he had for years and didn't anticipate the pressure the growth would put on the company's operational effectiveness. He didn't have his corporate "dashboard" to monitor the overall financial performance and operational effectiveness.

RPE is the critical number that must be on Frank's corporate dashboard. In addition, there are other measures that he will need to identify as well to have a fuller understanding of the operational effectiveness and to monitor how other areas are impacting his RPE.

THEIR DISCOVERY JOURNEY

"Frank, your morale issue is like that flashing warning light on your car dashboard. Right now, we don't have enough information to know if it is a minor issue or if you are on the verge of a catastrophic failure. It's obvious that you and Susan don't agree on how the company is performing. Both of you can't be correct," I said. "If you want the answer, we need more information, and you need to create your corporate dashboard."

Frank took a deep breath and said, "My gut tells me that we are in the Driving Zone, but I can't afford to be wrong. Tell us what you need."

Key Takeaways

○ What is your RPE? What is the trend over the past three to five years? If it is dropping, did you also indicate that you were in a Drama Zone at the end of Chapter 1?

○ How do you stack up against your industry's average RPE?

○ Pull your management team together and have them indicate on the Lifeline where they think the company is today. Are they in agreement, or do you have controversy?

○ If your RPE is stable and/or growing, what do you attribute that to? Increased sales? Decrease in number of employees? New systems?

○ If your RPE is dropping, why? New competition? Loss of customers? Adding employees to support high growth?

CHAPTER 3

Overheating

I wasn't quite sure how this meeting would go. Either Frank was going to be ready to roll up his sleeves, or he'd ask me to leave. This was going to be one of those leadership decisions directly affecting his company's Lifeline. Revenue per employee (RPE) is the critical number that measures effectiveness, but we also need to have an efficiency measurement to keep everything in balance. Otherwise, businesses will burn through their financial resources and, essentially, overheat.

It took Susan longer than expected to gather the information necessary for our next meeting. After rescheduling twice, we were finally ready to get back together. I walked into the office and followed the same instruction as before, dialing extension 107. This time, no one answered. I waited a couple minutes and tried again, but still no answer. As I took a seat and waited, I had a suspicion that the Drama was growing. About ten minutes later, Susan came around the corner and said apologetically, "Sorry to keep you waiting—our staff meeting ran long."

We went back into the same boardroom, and it hadn't changed much from the last meeting. Taking our same seats, we waited for Frank to arrive. "How are things going?" I asked. "Seems like the last couple weeks have been hectic."

Susan replied, "It has been the same Drama for me. One of the top engineers we hired last year from a large firm gave notice. He is going back to his prior company. It has caused some challenges, as we are having to move his work around to others who already have full plates."

"What are you going to do? Are you going to find a replacement?" I asked.

Giving a frustrated chuckle, she said, "We would have made that decision three weeks ago, but now, after gathering the information you requested, I've asked Frank if we could finish working with you before making any more hires."

Intrigued by her comments, I needed to know more. "I hope that means our work together is starting to bear fruit."

"It has," she replied. "After the last meeting, I wanted to know our revenue per employee, and I was astonished to see how much it has dropped over the past two years."

Before she could finish her thoughts, Frank walked in, apologizing for his tardiness. "Sorry, our staff meeting ran long and I needed to follow up on a few projects. I don't know if Susan told you or not, but one of our newer engineers gave notice last week, and we're making a few quick changes. He's a sharp guy and I hate to see him leave," he said.

I nodded my head. "Yes, Susan just told me. Did he give a reason for going back to his prior firm?"

"He's a very quiet and reserved guy, so he didn't say much to me." Frank turned to Susan. "What has he told you?"

Susan said reflectively, "John is always so quiet. It's really hard to get him to open up. He told me that he liked it here, but that it was a little too chaotic at times for him. He needs to work someplace where there's a lot of structure. I told him it would get better and encouraged him to stay, but his prior company made him an offer he said he couldn't pass up."

I had planned on jumping into the dashboard information that Susan had provided to me for the meeting, but I decided this was the perfect time to review part of the HR questionnaire that they had put together for me prior to the first meeting. This was a good opportunity to discuss one of the areas on the dashboard—employee management. Susan and Frank had completed the questionnaire independently, as I had asked, and the results were not surprising given the rapid change at the company.

I began, "Let's first start by reviewing the HR questionnaire. The tool is designed to help us understand where you are doing well and where you have room for improvement, and to help us identify the gaps. Both of you have unique perspectives, which is very helpful for our discussion. Frank, as the owner, you may not be getting the full story, as employees are afraid to tell you what they really think or what you need to know. However, Susan, in your role I would expect that you are closer to the day-to-day activities and more hands-on in your responses.

"Susan, how would you have described the morale of the company three years ago? What was it like to work around here?" I asked.

"Morale was good around here. It was like family. Many of us have worked together for years and watched children grow and employees get married, and also supported each other through the sad times. When my dad died about five years ago, everyone came to the funeral and was so supportive. It meant a lot to me," Susan explained. "Also, everyone knew what needed to get done each day. That's what made it hard for me to complete the questionnaire. I realized that a few years ago we didn't have much HR structure. In fact, HR was really just me managing the compliance and benefits. We all just worked together, and if something didn't work, we figured it out and kept going. We were a family—that's really the best way to put it."

I looked at Frank. "Would you agree with that?" I asked.

"Yes, we were like a family. I didn't see the need for a lot of structure," Frank said. "We all knew what needed to get done and we did it. If someone wasn't doing a good job, they'd eventually leave and we'd find someone to replace them who fit the culture better. One of the frustrating things today is that we've hired so many people, and with all the turnover I don't know everyone's name anymore. For example, in our staff meeting today there were faces there I don't think I've seen before."

"I believe we can come to an agreement on what is driving some of the challenges," I said. "From my review of the HR questionnaire, the company has grown substantially, but the HR infrastructure hasn't kept pace. It is common for companies to hire employees to meet the needs of business growth, but it is difficult to Go Slow and build the necessary infrastructure to support the growth."

> *Infrastructure is an important building block of business capability.*

I thought to myself: This is a great example of business growth outpacing business capability. Frank's company had evolved to meet the needs when it had thirty-five employees. Now, with over eighty employees, the business has many different needs that are not being met.

To illustrate for them, I reached into my bag and pulled out their responses to the questionnaire. "Let's look at how both of you answered the section on Effectiveness of Performance Management Practices," I started. "Frank, your answers are indicated in gray, and Susan, your answers are represented in black. From your answers, it appears that you both think you are about a three on a scale of one to five. What's interesting is that Frank made a circle from the top to the bottom, giving all of them a three. Susan, your answers are more specific."

Frank responded first, slightly annoyed. "I just assumed we were average. This was one of the sections that was difficult for me to complete. I only have a few people reporting to me anymore, so I'm somewhat removed from how well we're doing in these areas."

Susan chimed in, "This was difficult for me also. Technically, I am the HR person, but only by default. My primary duties are accounting. So, many of these things are left to the individual managers to do on their own. We don't have any formal training, so it was just a guess."

HOW EFFECTIVE ARE YOUR PERFORMANCE MANAGEMENT PRACTICES?

The Critical Components of an Effective Performance Management Plan	Rate Current Level of Effectiveness on a 1–5 Scale				
1. Giving tough, but necessary performance messages	1	(2)	3	4	5
2. Giving constructive feedback on a consistent basis	1	2	(3)	4	5
3. Giving stretch, but achievable goals	1	2	(3)	4	5
4. Breaking down goals into daily or weekly work plans	1	2	3	(4)	5
5. Handling difficult, but well-performing workers	1	2	(3)	4	5
6. Documenting poor performance	1	(2)	3	4	5
7. Capturing developmental insights	1	(2)	3	4	5
8. Following procedures on time	1	2	3	(4)	5
9. Separating "true" performance from personality	1	2	(3)	4	5
10. Encouraging employee involvement in performance improvement	1	2	(3)	4	5
Overall Level of Effectiveness:	10–20		20–35		35–50

"How would employees rate their managers? Would they give us the same answers? What if we asked the employee, John, who just resigned because he said he needs more structure?" I asked.

Frank, now growing aggravated, answered: "I hope they'd say we're doing a good job. We've been intentional about hiring new managers who have experience, and our tenured managers have been doing this a long time."

I looked at Susan, who seemed a little distraught as she answered: "When I think about all of the questions I get from managers and the rumors and complaints from employees, I think they'd probably give us low scores." Looking at Frank, she continued, "Maybe this is part of the reason that John resigned last week.

"This is why I feel like we're in the Drama Zone. It seems that every day I have another issue coming to me from the managers. We don't have consistency among them, and it is creating issues," she said. "In fact, there's a rumor that we don't expect as much from our newer employees. I don't think that's true, but it's how some of our long-term employees feel."

The conversation didn't seem to be sitting too well with Frank, as if it had struck a nerve. Pausing for a moment to collect himself, he turned to me and said, "Apparently we're not doing as well as I thought. I've been so focused on growing the company, and I may have assumed that everyone would just know what to do. It looks like you've given me the answer I was looking for on how to solve our morale issue. We need to put in place management training and then establish clear expectations for the staff."

Frank was growing impatient and was looking to move to a quick resolution of what he now viewed as the underlying reason for the morale problems he had called me to help him fix.

To help Frank and Susan put these concepts together, I drew three images on the whiteboard. The first was the Lifeline chart, next to it the four stages of competence, and finally a rough image of a car dashboard with two circles inside.

Performance and Time

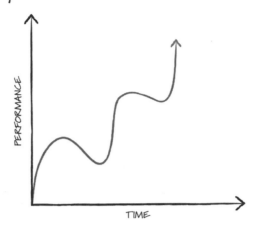

Stages of Competence

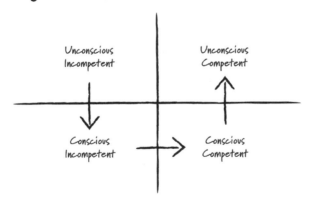

Dashboard

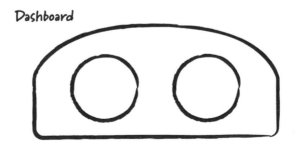

"Forgive me," I began, "but I believe there is more to it than merely improving the company's employee management practices. Let's review our discussion so far." I pointed to the Lifeline. "First, we talked about where you thought your company was on the Lifeline. You indicated that it was in the Driving Zone, and Susan felt it was in the Drama Zone." I marked where they had indicated. "We discussed the differences between the Driving Zone and the Drama Zone. The Driving Zone is where the company is running smoothly, and the Drama Zone is where the company has outgrown its underlying business capability and issues arise. To get out of a Drama Zone, a business has to Go Slow and make changes that allow it to support the growth." I drew a circle around each part of a trough in the Lifeline.

"Then we discussed the four stages of competence. This helps us make sure we are asking the right questions." Turning to the two of them, I asked, "Which stage has the most risk?"

Frank and Susan discussed it between themselves and Frank turned and said, "It must be stage 1, where you don't know what you don't know.

"Perfect, and which stage is the highest performing?"

Frank answered quickly, "Well, that would have to be stage 4, where the business is unconsciously competent."

Then, moving over to the dashboard, I said, "Remember my analogy of the driver? He didn't immediately get to stage 4 when he got his driver's license. He had to go through stages 2 and 3 to get to 4." I drew arrows in each of the zones. "Yet, the car's dashboard was there the entire time. He just hadn't developed the skills and knowledge to know how to use all of the information.

"We agreed that in order to see where you were on the Lifeline, we needed to create your company's dashboard. The first gauge I asked about was revenue per employee," I said as I wrote "RPE" in one of the circles. "This is only a simple metric, but it does give us important information about *effectiveness*."

> *Effectiveness and efficiency are words commonly misunderstood or misused. Simply, effectiveness means producing a desired result while efficiency means producing a desired result with fewer resources.*

I wrote "ROI" in the other circle. To emphasize my point, I circled ROI multiple times. "This is another very important but easy metric—return on investment. ROI measures your *efficiency*. These two are foundational. Used together, they provide you with the basic information to determine your business's *capability*. Effectiveness and efficiency are words commonly misunderstood or misused. Simply, effectiveness means producing a desired result while efficiency means producing a desired result with fewer resources."

I drew a few more circles in the dashboard and told them that we would fill these gauges in with the information they provided. In one circle, I wrote "Morale."

I looked at Frank and said, "I agree with your observation that we need to improve the employee management and establish clear expectations. This will have an impact on morale. But I hope you see that is only one part of building a high-performance company."

Frank smiled and managed a chuckle. "I was hoping this was going to be easy."

| *What doesn't get measured doesn't get done.*

DRIVING EFFICIENCY

Frank, with Susan's help, had built a very successful company and had achieved the results through their close involvement with the company. As the company grew over the years, they were small enough to have a day-to-day understanding of the issues and challenges. They could adjust as necessary, and the entire staff worked like a family. As the company grew quickly over the past couple of years, they continued to run the company in much the same way, except with more people. Frank anticipated the challenges and attempted to hire experienced people to help manage the growth.

Frank was beginning to understand. He didn't know what he didn't know.

To build a high-performing company, it is necessary to strive to keep business *growth* and business *capability* in alignment. A skilled leader learns that this is both an art and a skill. The ability to monitor results and anticipate the future, making modifications and changes, is critical for staying in the Driving Zone and mitigating or avoiding Drama Zones.

The first tool for monitoring results gave us information on effectiveness—revenue per employee. But it isn't enough to only measure top line results. We also need a tool to measure efficiency. For this we will use return on investment.

ROI is a metric that calculates the efficiency of an investment. It is commonly used when comparing one simple investment to another. For example, let's suppose you invested $1,000 in a stock and then sold it a year later for $1,200. You would calculate your ROI by dividing your gain of $200 ($1,200–$1,000) by your purchase price of $1,000 ($200/$1,000), resulting in an ROI of 20 percent. In contrast, if you invested $2,000 in a stock and sold it a year later for $2,300, your gain would be $300, but at a lower ROI of 15 percent ($300/$2,000). Thus the first investment generated the higher ROI and would be considered a more efficient investment.

Similarly, businesses often make decisions on new purchases or investments by calculating the ROI to see how quickly the purchase will get paid back through either decreased costs or increased efficiencies. For example, a business may consider replacing all of their incandescent light bulbs with energy-efficient LED lights. The investment may include replacing ballasts and other upgrades that increase the costs beyond just the increased cost of the light bulbs. However, over time the decrease in energy costs greatly outweighs the investment and will save money and increase profits over the long run. This makes it an efficient investment.

Businesses make significant investments in property, plant, and equipment to operate their businesses. These investments in hard assets are easily identifiable, and the decision making involved will be based on targeted outcomes that may include product quality, processing speed, accessibility, location, and life expectancy, while also pursuing a positive ROI. Over time, businesses typically assess, review, and make changes to their property, plant, and equipment with the goal of ensuring that they meet the ongoing demands on the company efficiently and effectively while also competing for customers and their money.

The speed of business today, however, can often quickly make these decisions obsolete. For example, Blockbuster's strategy to rent videos at over nine thousand retail locations at its peak was knocked off by Netflix's direct-to-your-door shipping and Redbox's inexpensive distribution kiosks. The retail store distribution channel became a very expensive underlying cost per video rental compared to the new disruptive technologies. Thus, the ROI for Blockbuster on their retail stores plummeted with the drop in prices from their new lower-cost competitors. It is safe to say that Blockbuster was in the Driving Zone at their peak but ended up going into the Drama Zone and ultimately business death by not anticipating and making the changes in their business capability necessary to survive.

THE KEY TO HIGH PERFORMANCE

In today's business world, it isn't enough merely to maximize the ROI on capital investments such as production equipment, technology, and systems. Today businesses must also maximize their return on what, for most companies, is their largest expenditure—people. It is perplexing that the largest expense for most businesses is the hardest to manage, the most highly regulated, and the least planned.

The challenge is that businesses accumulate practices and precedents related to employees over time. Many companies are straddled with decisions made when they were small that become cumbersome, expensive, or out-of-date as they grow.

For example, one of the businesses that I coached made the decision to pay 100 percent of the cost of health care benefits for their employees and their families when they were a small business. Most of the employees were single, and a key employee was the only one on family coverage. This was a very nice benefit to offer the employees, but it wasn't necessarily expensive given the size of the company and how many were actually enrolled in the benefits. As the company grew, however, employees got married, new employees with families were hired, and the overall cost became prohibitive. The company had to make some hard decisions going forward to reduce the overall costs. Unfortunately, they were growing quickly and this was difficult to change in the middle of the fiscal year.

This is a simple example of costs that can quickly escalate and significantly impact the ROI per person. There are many more examples that are less obvious and provide significant risk. For example, a small chemical engineering company of about twenty employees promoted a female employee from receptionist to marketing manager and ultimately to director of sales and marketing over many years. She was given this title not based on internal factors, skills, or duties, but to help her increase her image to potential customers. Unfortunately, the company began to struggle financially and decided to let her go. In retaliation, she filed suit for wage discrimination because the male director of chemical research earned about $50,000 more a year than she did. Because the business didn't have job descriptions, the owner couldn't provide evidence to defend the compensation difference, so he settled the lawsuit for $100,000. This was a tough financial pill to swallow when the company was struggling to survive. The owner didn't have the legal knowledge to know that he put his company at financial risk for discrimination.

> *The owner didn't have the legal knowledge to know that he put his company at financial risk for discrimination.*

Do you have blind spots putting your company at risk that could easily be fixed?

Often the decisions that companies make are in direct correlation with the size of the company, and by virtue of their size tend to have very similar characteristics.

CHARACTERISTICS BY SIZE

Start-up to twenty employees

- No job descriptions
- Highly motivated employees
- High commitment
- Limited employee benefits
- Ad hoc decision making

Twenty to fifty employees

- Structure becomes more important
- Pressures on employee benefits
- Motivation varies
- Time management incrementally harder
- Some management layers
- Increase in outside vendors
- Recruiting through referrals

Fifty to two hundred employees

- Organizational structure a necessity
- Pay/performance inequities affect morale
- Decision rights by role are a necessity
- Recruiting becomes more professional
- Employee liability exposure increases

- Motivation varies significantly

- Employee retention becomes very important

- Morale building efforts begin

- Weak managers can no longer hide

To complicate matters, management's decisions on organizational structure are most often reactive rather than proactive. Thus, what works when the company has fifteen employees isn't appropriate for a company of eighty employees.

It was obvious to me early in our initial meeting that Frank was still running his business like he did when he had thirty-five employees. His Get It Done work ethic worked when he had a small group of highly committed employees. However, it was like a warning light on the dashboard that he had a problem. He had not evolved the overall management style to meet the needs of the business as it grew.

Unlike an investment in software or machinery that can improve performance when installed, improving the ROI of employees requires a comprehensive human resource management strategy that will take time to implement and deliver results.

Containing or reducing costs is an important component in increasing ROI, but there is another component that has a significant impact on ROI: increasing the effectiveness per person by improving an employee's skills and abilities which then should lead to the overall ability of the company to generate more revenue with fewer employees. Increasing effectiveness is much more complicated and requires an ongoing comprehensive plan for maintaining peak levels of morale and motivation, and ultimately bringing employees to their full potential.

The key is to continuously improve effectiveness while simultaneously containing costs, in an organized and structured manner that meets the current needs and prepares the organization for the future. This strategy will include items such as processing platform, regulatory management, compensation and benefits design, performance management, and training and development.

By managing both effectiveness and costs, businesses are on the path to maximizing ROI per person. In order to do this, management needs to understand where they are today and what initiatives will improve both.

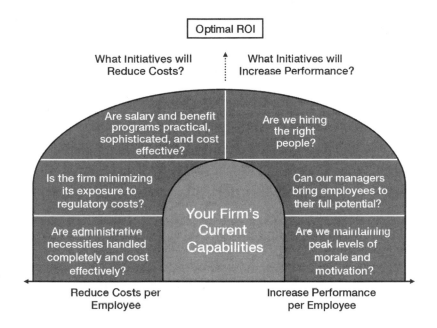

It is baffling why businesses will spend substantial resources and decision making on property, plant, and equipment to increase efficiency but don't put the same effort toward planning to increase the efficiency of their largest investment—people.

In Frank's case, he ran his company like a lifestyle business, without much human resource management structure. As the company doubled in size, the lack of structure began to show early warning signs. Frank anticipated challenges and hired experienced managers and professionals, but what else did he do to prepare his company for the future? Did he identify out-of-date, inadequate, or expensive policies? Did he implement training to quickly bring his new employees to full performance? Did he provide his management team with the information and tools to manage performance? In short, did he Go Slow to prepare his company to Grow Fast?

> *High-performing businesses maximize their return on investment by efficiently increasing effectiveness per person.*

THE NUMBERS DON'T LIE

Frank was discovering that you can't rely on your gut to know how your business is operating. He and Susan were learning the importance of using RPE to measure effectiveness and ROI to measure efficiency. Together these provide management with critical numbers that measure the results of their cumulative decisions. Deep down, Frank was beginning to realize that maybe Susan was right and he was wrong. Maybe they were in a Drama Zone. He was becoming dimly aware that he had not prepared his organization for growth. My next step was to shine a bright light on his current situation.

It was clear to me that Frank didn't know what he didn't know, but he was about to find out.

Key Takeaways

○ What things should you stop doing or start doing with regard to personnel management? What practices have you accumulated that may have been OK when you were smaller but negatively impact the business today?

○ Is your personnel management aligned with the size of your company today? What about the future? If you are growing at 20 percent a year, what are you doing to proactively maintain alignment?

○ Are your personnel expenses your largest expense (other than cost of goods sold)? What are you doing to maximize the ROI on this investment?

○ What do you still feel you need to learn? Is there anything you feel like you are unsure of?

CHAPTER 4

Into the Garage

Entrepreneurs and business leaders have all faced that point where they have been thrilled with their success and growth but one day wake up to realize that the next increment of growth is more challenging and less profitable. Most leaders would never want to admit it, but most likely this is a result of their lack of planning and execution for the future. Frank wasn't any different. Frank hadn't yet realized that his company had hit its proverbial growth ceiling—that point at which the company's growth had exceeded its organizational capability. From this point forward, every percentage point in growth was met with resistance, challenge, and frustration. In other words, Frank's company was in the Drama Zone.

My original suspicions about Frank's challenges from his initial email were correct. On the surface, his morale problem was a by-product of his high growth and the cultural resistance. But the deeper reality was that the company had outgrown the underlying organizational capability. He had hit the growth ceiling. From the beginning, Frank and Susan were in disagreement about whether the company was in the Driving Zone or Drama Zone on the Lifeline. Frank was running the company based on gut feeling, and Susan was living the daily financial and personnel Drama. To get on the same page, they needed a dashboard to monitor their organizational effectiveness and efficiency. During our first couple of meetings, we were able to gain perspective, and now we were ready to look at their numbers and lay out a plan for the future. It was time to help them burst through the ceiling—to prepare them to Grow Fast.

Like many entrepreneurs I have met, Frank was self-confident and driven. He had a natural competitive nature that I noticed from the moment we met. This was further supported by the boardroom's collection of awards, plaques, and recognitions that the company and Frank had received over the years. I had also learned during our meetings that Frank, not a patient person, liked to control the situation and wanted to get immediate results. He had asked me to help him solve a morale problem, and now he was facing something much more significant—he was beginning to realize that he didn't know what he didn't know. His company was deep into a Drama Zone and he didn't know it.

It was time to get into the numbers.

"Let's review a couple of the highlights of the report," I said. "First, your revenue per employee has dropped significantly over the past few years. Five years ago, you were averaging about $110,000 per employee, and then about three years ago it began dropping, and now is around $80,000. This means your company's effectiveness has dropped around 30 percent. In my opinion, RPE is the most critical number for every business, as it is the ultimate measure of effectiveness. When a company has a drop in RPE, it is an early warning sign that the company could be entering a Drama Zone."

Taking a deep breath, Frank sighed and said, "This is disturbing, but I'm not surprised. We've grown so fast that we've had to add employees based on our increase in clients and projects. So we've been hiring ahead of the revenue. Are you telling me that we shouldn't have done that? Because if we didn't, we wouldn't have had the staff to meet the needs of our clients."

"No," I said, "in a period of high growth it's often necessary to hire employees ahead of the revenue. However, as we'll discuss later, there are best practices that will soften the impact of growth.

"Next," I continued, "is your return on investment on your staff. The money you pay your staff is much like a financial investment. The goal is to maximize the ROI. By dividing your net profit by your total cost of compensation, we can calculate your staff's ROI. As you can see from the report, over the past three years your ROI has dropped significantly.

"This is partly related to the increase in staff we just discussed; however, while reviewing your details I found that other factors have also contributed to this drop in ROI," I said. "For example, I noticed that your average wage has increased by 10 percent. This was mostly related to the increase in your management team and their respective wages. Also, I noticed that your benefits costs have risen dramatically. These are just a couple of the factors I noticed, but there are others we can address as well."

Susan, who had been quietly reviewing the information, looked distraught. I asked what was on her mind.

Looking up over her reading glasses, she looked like she might start crying. "I feel responsible for these results," she said. "As the controller, my job is to manage our finances, and I've let Frank down. I know that our expenses have grown and that we've had a lot of pressure about meeting the needs of our clients, but I'm also the HR person, and based on these numbers I feel like I've let the company down on both finances and personnel. Sometimes I feel over my head as we grow. There's only so much time in a day, and sometimes I feel defeated, like today."

Trying to lighten the moment and hoping to be a little witty, I said dryly, "Well, it looks like you picked the right guy to help you with your company's morale. I've certainly lifted your spirits. Who's next?"

Both Frank and Susan laughed.

Frank was now smiling, but still serious. "Actually, you are helping," he said. "Susan has been telling me adamantly for months that our expenses have really grown and that our profits are down. I've kept telling her that it was OK, because growth is expensive and that we would be fine and grow out of it. It has put a lot of pressure on our relationship, and to be candid it has become strained over the past year. Her morale has suffered, and I just keep telling her to keep her chin up."

"Let's move on with the report," I said. "ROI and RPE are important primary indicators, but let's look at more of the results to get a deeper understanding of the challenge before us. On the next page are more data points over the past three years. The growth rate has been impressive, and you've more than doubled your employees, office space, and management team. Also, you've added two more layers of management. All in all, you've made significant investments to support your growth. However, there are some troubling numbers. First, your employee turnover rate has almost tripled, your employee average tenure has dropped significantly, and your client retention has a negative trend."

	TWO YEARS PRIOR	PRIOR YEAR	MOST RECENT YEAR
Growth rate	32%	35%	36%
Office space	7,000 sq ft	15,000 sq ft	20,000 sq ft
Number of managers/ supervisors	4	6	10
Layers of management	2	2	4
Number of employees	35	52	80
Employee turnover	5%	11%	13%
Employee average tenure	8.7 years	4.5 years	2.8 years
Client retention	91%	88%	84%

Frank was now more visibly troubled. His body language said it all. With hands clasped together under his chin, he studied the information in front of him. His normal confidence seemed shaken.

"These data points further support what the RPE and ROI data revealed," I said. "They tell an interesting story. At a high level, this is how I interpret this data: You've had great top line growth success that put pressure on the company to expand facilities, people, and management. However, contrary to my motto of 'Go Slow to Grow Fast,' the company's business capability wasn't prepared for the significant growth, as indicated by the increase in turnover, drop in average tenure, and ultimately loss of clients. Most likely, the drop in morale is a by-product of all of these things."

If there was any positive energy remaining in the room, it seemed to leave both Frank and Susan at this point.

Looking back and forth at Frank and Susan, I said, "The good news is that you have a great company with talented people and a strong leader. The expanded, experienced management team most likely helped support the growth and limit the downside. In other words, if you hadn't added seasoned professionals to the company then the results could have been much worse. We need to develop your strategic plan to move the company to the Driving Zone and develop your dashboard so that you can monitor and anticipate challenges in the future.

"Are you prepared to start this journey?" I asked.

Frank responded first. "Absolutely—I didn't grow this company to fail. But how do we do it quickly? We are very busy right now, and I don't know how I can take the time to fix so many things."

Susan, who had been very quiet, finally spoke up. "I think we can do this with some structure and planning. We have a good management team that needs direction. I really feel relieved to understand my gut feelings. My gut told me we were in the Drama Zone, but I just couldn't put it all together. Now I believe that with some guidance I can help us move in the right direction."

I was thrilled that they were both committed to moving forward. I knew Frank would want fast results, but they would need a road map to get there. Also, they needed to know that what they were facing was not easy. It was going to take a commitment of time to Go Slow and strategically think, plan, and execute in preparation to Grow Fast. Frank had made some smart decisions to support the company's growth, adding experienced staff and beginning to build out the management team. He would see that these were critical components that would help us move more quickly. It was now time to introduce my Quad 4 methodology to them.

I stood up and went back to the whiteboard and drew a new matrix, labeling the vertical line ROI and the horizontal line Effectiveness, with Low and High at opposite ends. Turning around, I said, "Let's plot ROI against RPE. Susan, on the sheet in front of you, can you tell me the ROI from three years ago?"

Susan looked down at the report in front of her and said, "It looks like our ROI was around 10 percent."

"Would you consider that to be high or low based on your history?" I asked her.

Susan took a few moments and flipped through a financial statement binder she had in front of her and said, "That was one of our more profitable years, so I would say it was high."

I made a mark on the ROI line in the High section and labeled it 2013. "Now, how about the RPE?" I asked. "How would you rate the company's effectiveness in that same year?"

Anticipating my next question, she said, "Using RPE to measure effectiveness, it was $100,000 per employee, and if I compare that to five years ago, I would rank it as low." I then made a mark on the Low side of the effectiveness line and labeled it 2013. I plotted the two data points with an X.

"Let's call this Quad 1," I said, as I wrote that on the board. "Let's do the same thing for this last year. How would you rank both ROI and RPE?" I asked.

Looking over her reading glasses at me, Susan sighed and said, "They would both be low. Our ROI was less than 1 percent and our RPE dropped to $80,000."

I grabbed a red marker from the whiteboard shelf and made a red mark to the left of where 2013 was marked and another red mark on the Low side of the ROI line. I plotted these two marks and made an X. "Let's call this Quad 2," I said, and I finished by naming the remaining two sections Quad 3 and Quad 4.

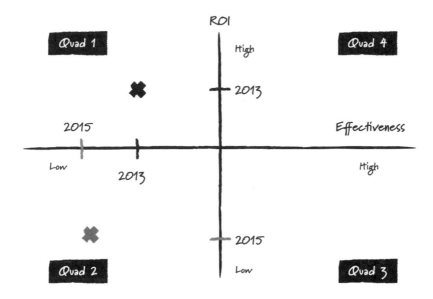

QUAD 4 METHODOLOGY

This matrix assesses a business's maturity on two dimensions. The first dimension looks at how the business is **financially** performing and the second dimension looks at how the business is **operationally** performing.

What I have discovered is that businesses in Quad 1 are oftentimes in the initial stages of entering a Drama Zone. These businesses have hit their growth ceiling—the point where their growth has exceeded their organizational capability. As companies move into Quad 2, they often are squarely in a Drama Zone, focusing on fixing problems and issues that come from a lack of effective planning and execution. Those businesses in Quad 3 are Going Slow, focused on sacrificing profitability for long-term effectiveness. Finally, Quad 4 businesses are maximizing both profits and effectiveness, resulting in a high-performance business ready to Grow Fast.

IMPORTANT NOTE: RPE is a simple measure-ment of effectiveness, but it isn't the only measure. Overall effectiveness is much more complicated to measure and must take into account both input and output measurements.

Frank was now out of his seat and walking toward the white-board. He grabbed a green marker and made a big X in the top right corner of Quad 4 and said, "This is where I want to go. What do we have to do to get there?"

I smiled at Frank's reaction. It was as if it finally hit him that his company was heading in the wrong direction and he couldn't control himself to sit still. In fact, he now seemed to understand the path I was taking him down.

"Frank, that is exactly where we want to go. We want to get your company into Quad 4," I said. "To begin with, let's put together a simple list of the items that affect RPE and ROI," I said, as I erased part of the whiteboard and wrote "RPE" and "ROI" in two columns.

Susan jumped in. "Under RPE there would be increased prices, increased sales, and new products and services, and under ROI there would be staff reductions, lower contributions to benefits, and lower administrative support costs," she rattled off as Frank quickly scribbled these on the whiteboard.

Frank continued to write as he said, "For RPE, how about increased client retention? If I think about the clients we've lost over fifteen years, we could be three times bigger than we are today. We have good retention, but if it were better, that would increase revenue. It takes us a long time to get a new client, and they are expensive to replace. So now that I think about it, retention would also improve our ROI, as our costs to service are lower and more profitable the longer we work with a company. We understand how to work together and their nuances."

"Both of you are correct—these are just a few of the many things that impact RPE and ROI," I said. "Of course, as you just identified, Frank, often they are interconnected. The challenge is that some things improve both ROI and RPE, but others work against each other. For example, you can increase prices, but will that decrease sales? However, the increased profit margin on the higher prices might be more profitable, as you may not need as many employees to serve the higher profit margin business."

Frank laughed. "OK, now my head is spinning. I'm an engineer, not an MBA. I need a blueprint and a plan," he said as he took his seat again.

"This simple matrix is what we'll use to lay out the blueprint or plan for the future," I said. "I call it Quad 4. It is my methodology to help provide businesses such as yours a systemic process for the pursuit of a high-performance business. From the data you provided, I would have plotted your company in Quad 4 five years ago. You were enjoying solid profits and high RPE. As you can see by the way we plotted your company, you moved into Quad 1 in 2013, and then by 2015 you had moved into Quad 2. Our goal now is to help you Go Slow and assess those things that you can do over the next one to two years that will move you into Quad 4 again. But more importantly, we need to build your dashboard so that you can monitor your business to make timely decisions to smooth out your company Lifeline.

"The good news is that you intuitively anticipated the pressures on your business and hired experienced professionals and began making changes to your business to help meet the demands of your growth," I said. "In fact, I believe we will be able to move you to

Quad 4 much quicker than other businesses that I have worked with because of the manner in which you approach running your business.

"To help explain, let me tell you a story about another client of mine that faced a similar challenge," I continued. "They'd enjoyed a lot of growth, but unlike you, when I met them they hadn't made investments in their management team. In fact, not only had they not improved their staff, but they'd also failed to improve many of their underlying systems and processes. For example, their accounting system was antiquated, using software designed for simple bookkeeping. They were using spreadsheets to track much of their sales and customer information, and they lacked integration and had silos of data. From a growth and profit perspective, they had success, but they were starting to have cash flow problems, and the owner, James, couldn't understand why his financials showed that he was profitable but also tight on cash. That's why he called me to help. Because of the growth, he'd exhausted his line of credit at his bank, and they were asking questions he couldn't answer.

"Not only had James failed to improve his underlying information systems, but he'd also neglected improving and developing his staff. As we began digging into his company, we found that his employee turnover was horrible, at almost 35 percent over a couple of years. He'd lost a few good people, and those who had been with him for a long time kept getting promoted as the organization grew because they were good at their current job. It was a classic example of the management theory known as the Peter Principle, which describes individuals being promoted beyond their highest level of competence. Even basic employee management items were out of date or didn't exist. The employee handbook had been copied many years earlier from a handbook borrowed from a friend. It was severely out of date and didn't fit their unique needs. They didn't train managers on the basics of employment laws, and that was obvious when I sat through an interview a manager had with a prospective employee.

"Simply put, the company's financial statements didn't tell the whole story. We uncovered the source of the cash flow problems, but we also discovered that the owner's business philosophy was that he 'saved money to make money.' Each decision he made seemed to be about how he could spend as little as possible to maximize his profits. James's business was in Quad 1. He was pushing as much out of his company as he could, and it was on the brink of failure.

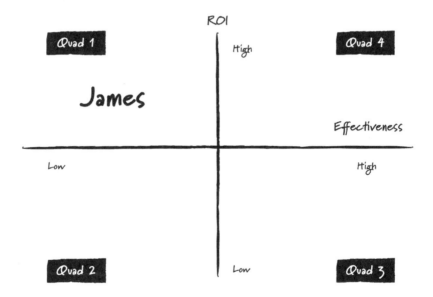

"Quad 1 businesses maximize their financial performance by avoiding spending time and/or money on the business's infrastructure and effectiveness. In other words, they don't invest to improve the company's business capability and ultimately the resulting performance. The financial statements for these companies may look like they're doing well, but when analyzing their business capability we find that they're in a high-risk area of failure or future problems—because they're not investing in *effectiveness*."

Frank was deep in thought at this point. He turned to me and said, "Let me make sure I get this straight. What you're saying is that the key to high performance is continuously improving effectiveness while also controlling costs. That makes perfect sense, but these seem to be in conflict with each other. If I invest to improve effectiveness, my costs will increase and impact my overall profitability, but if I only focus on profitability I will put my business at risk."

"Yes, that's why it's critical to Go Slow—to understand where you are today so that we can identify the activities and tactics that will make the biggest difference the quickest," I said. "We can easily monitor your ROI, but we need to set goals and targets to measure and improve your effectiveness. We also need to know your growth plans for the future. Because, as we discussed before, the faster you grow, the more pressure it puts on your company's effectiveness. That's why growth is so expensive. There's pressure on businesses to hire more employees, but if they don't Go Slow and improve their underlying systems, they're making things worse.

"We're now on a path toward putting together your dashboard. Remember our discussion about the stages of competence?" I asked. "Let's put the two matrixes next to one another and see what similarities you see."

Frank and Susan quietly studied the two matrixes. Susan was the first to speak up. "It seems to me," she said, "that the Unconscious Incompetence stage is similar to Quad 1. If you are in Quad 1, you probably don't know what you don't know. Both have high risk. And if you are in the Unconscious Competence stage, then you are in Quad 4, because you have all the information you need to unconsciously make decisions and perform the highest."

Smiling, I raised my hand in a fist to my mouth as if it were a microphone and said, "We have a winner," and then pretended to do a microphone drop. We all laughed. "That's it, and it's why we must put together your dashboard so that you can unconsciously and competently run the business."

DRIVING PERFORMANCE

Getting to and staying in Quad 4 is a very difficult management challenge. However, those businesses that continuously pursue this goal will smooth out their business Lifeline, as they will anticipate and mitigate the Drama Zones by making timely changes in their business.

Getting to and staying in Quad 4 is a very difficult management challenge. However, those businesses that continuously pursue this goal will smooth out their business Lifeline.

To accurately assess their group, businesses will need both quantitative and qualitative data similar to the data identified for Frank and Susan. This information helps management understand where they would plot themselves in the matrix and provides the foundation for future decision making and results monitoring.

Yet, even without the specific data, I have found that there are general characteristics about businesses that tend to indicate in which group they are operating.

	IT/OPERATION SYSTEMS	PERSONNEL MANAGEMENT	BUSINESS PLANNING	FINANCIAL FOCUS	OPERATIONAL FOCUS	DASHBOARD
QUAD 1	Disparate	Ad hoc	Little to none	Profits	Spend as little as possible	None
QUAD 2	Disparate	Ad hoc	Little to none	Cash flow	Focus on problem solving	None
QUAD 3	Partially integrated	Basic processes	At least annually	Long term	Investing in systems and people	Basic
QUAD 4	Integrated	Comprehensive HR management	Ongoing	Focus on increasing ROI and RPE	Self-learning and improving organization	Comprehensive

Most business leaders can quickly and accurately place themselves based on the way they run their business. It comes down to their views on driving profits and effectiveness. Are they focused on saving money to make money? Is employee training and development important? Do they have a high risk tolerance for the unknown? Have they developed organizations that self-improve? Do they invest in technology and systems to improve timeliness and accuracy? Do they measure customer satisfaction? Overall, what is their business's operational effectiveness?

Important Point

The paradox between the Lifeline and the Quad 4 matrix is that a business leader may subjectively believe they are in the Driving Zone and thus must also be in Quad 4, but the reality is that the Driving Zone could be either Quad 1 or 4 and the Drama Zone could be either Quad 2 or 3. In other words, businesses that only judge their performance based on profitability see only half of the picture. It is critical that they also Go Slow and assess their organizational effectiveness—to fully understand the challenge before them and to provide the information necessary to balance growth with capability and ensure they are poised to Grow Fast.

Paradox between Lifeline and Quad 4 Matrix

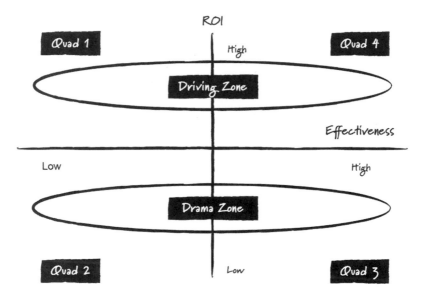

QUAD 1 (HIGH ROI AND LOW EFFECTIVENESS)

Businesses can find themselves in Quad 1 either intentionally or unintentionally. Some leaders intentionally place more importance on profitability than sustainability. They are focused on making money and do everything they can to keep overhead down. Among the indicators that a business is in Quad 1 is that the leaders bend the rules to keep down costs. For example, they may treat people as independent contractors instead of hiring them as employees to avoid costs and risks, yet if the IRS came knocking the problems would begin. Also, to save money, they don't offer employee benefits such as health insurance, which does save money but also greatly limits the ability to attract and retain employees. On the other hand, some businesses end up in Quad 1 unintentionally. These businesses often outgrow their capability but are unaware of it until problems surface. This would be like the Unconscious Incompetence stage discussed earlier. They don't know that the business's organizational effectiveness is inadequate to meet their needs.

QUAD 2 (LOW ROI AND LOW EFFECTIVENESS)

Businesses in Quad 2 are in repair mode as they recognize that they are experiencing problems and issues that must be fixed. For example, they might experience a loss of key employees, increased mistakes and errors, a drop in employee morale, shrinking profits, etc. The business leader realizes that in order for the business to continue to grow and thrive, they have some problems to fix, and the business starts spending money that it hadn't before. One of the more common examples is the hiring of the company's first HR person. The company has gotten by as long as it could without an HR person and then they get hit with that first employment lawsuit—and then all those years of getting by without clearly established guidelines and policies comes back to hit them in the form of legal fees and settlement costs.

QUAD 3 (LOW ROI AND HIGH EFFECTIVENESS)

Businesses in Quad 3 are Going Slow. They are sacrificing their ROI to increase the long-term success of the business by investing in effectiveness—spending time and money to improve both systems and people. The system improvements will provide the foundational support to meet the current and future growth of the organization, and this, coupled with the investment in their people, will drive increasing revenue per employee in the long term. These businesses have learned the importance of continuously improving their operational effectiveness and are willing to sacrifice to move into Quad 4: prepared to Grow Fast.

QUAD 4 (HIGH ROI AND HIGH EFFECTIVENESS)

These businesses are the envy of their competitors, as they continuously enjoy higher profit margins, growth, and success. They have created systems and people that provide exceptional products and services. Their operational platforms, people, and strategy keep them ahead of the competition. Their higher profit margins allow them to continuously pursue new products and services, expanding their markets and success. Their dashboard measurements provide them with information that allows them to make timely adjustments to the business. While not every company has a dashboard, it is an essential tool in providing knowledge about where the company is within its Lifeline.

THE REALITY OF THE QUADS

The reality is that businesses over time will find themselves in different Quads. A company may have ideal systems and people at $5 million in revenue and identify as a Quad 4 business, but then grow to $10 million in revenue, outgrowing their effectiveness and finding themselves in Quad 1 or 2. Oftentimes businesses won't recognize that they have entered Quad 1, as they continue to generate high ROI but don't recognize that their organizational effectiveness hasn't kept up with their growth until problems arise. They have hit their growth ceiling, and this begins the Drama cycle. The business begins having problems, and management doesn't fully understand the challenge ahead of them. They begin spending money to repair the issues and problems, and as a result they enter Quad 2. Over time, they identify the problems and begin making longer-term corrections that move them into Quad 3 with the goal of getting back to Quad 4.

Getting to Quad 4

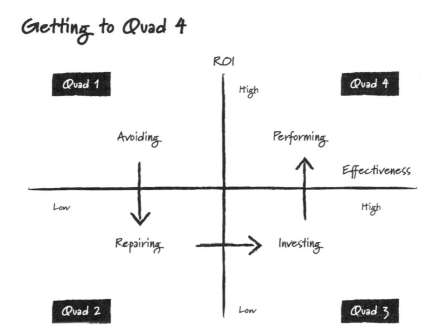

This is what happened with Frank's business. At thirty-five employees, he was a Quad 4 business, but as he grew, he didn't realize that his organizational effectiveness hadn't kept up with the growth. He began hiring more experienced professionals to help with the growth, but he didn't improve the overall organizational effectiveness to meet the needs of the larger company. This revealed itself when he realized he had an employee morale issue.

THE POWER OF 10 TO 1

"Before we build your dashboard, there is one more important point that we must discuss," I said. "Both of you seem to understand the importance of ROI and RPE, but let me tell you a secret. I call it the Power of 10 to 1. When you decrease costs, it only provides a 1-to-1 financial benefit—save a dollar, and that savings drops to the bottom line. However, the real key to success is improving your effectiveness, because a 1 percent increase in effectiveness drops 10 percent to the bottom line!"

This usually gets a business owner's attention.

Key Takeaways

○ Quad 4 is the business tool that measures the sum of all of your decisions as a leader over time. By continuously monitoring RPE and ROI against each other, you are able to accurately depict where you are on the Lifeline. It also provides you with information to lead your management team, as they will understand the reasons for the decisions made.

○ Where did you place yourself in the Quads? Are you in Quad 3 and intentionally making investments to improve your organizational effectiveness? Or do you think you are in Quad 4 but need to validate because you could actually be in Quad 1?

○ What decisions can you make that will move you more quickly into Quad 4 (or stay in Quad 4)?

○ Remember the paradox between the Lifeline and the Quads. You need factual data to properly determine your location.

○ What is your growth ceiling? Have you already hit it, or how close are you to hitting it?

CHAPTER 5

Finding the Gears

I always tell business leaders that saving money is not the long-term key to prosperity. Instead, it is the proper balance of cost containment and investment that drives success. The key is to shift gears in the proper sequence to maximize results.

"You have my attention now!" Frank said. "How can a 1 percent increase in effectiveness increase profitability 10 percent? That just doesn't seem possible. But if it's true, then the quickest way to get to Quad 4 is by focusing on increasing our effectiveness by 10 percent, and that will give us a 100 percent increase in profitability."

10-1 is the key to building a high-performance company.

"Great question, so let's walk through the logic," I said. On the whiteboard, I created a summarized income statement and wrote in comparative financial information for two years.

	YEAR 1	YEAR 2	CHANGE
Gross Profit	$10 million	$10.1 million	1%
Expenses	$9 million	$9 million	—
Net Profit	$1 million	$1.1 million	10%

"In this example, the company generated $10 million in gross profit in year 1, and if they can increase their effectiveness in gross revenue by 1 percent in year 2, it will increase to $10.1 million. If they can do this and keep expenses the same, their net profit will increase by 10 percent," I explained. "So, you would be correct: if you can increase effectiveness by 10 percent, your net profit will increase 100 percent if you can do it without increasing expenses." I updated the numbers on the chart to reflect the 10 percent increase in gross profit to illustrate for them.

	YEAR 1	YEAR 2	CHANGE
Gross Profit	$10 million	$11 million	10%
Expenses	$9 million	$9 million	—
Net Profit	$1 million	$2 million	100%

"The challenge is how to increase effectiveness without increasing expenses," I continued. "Or, another way to think about it is this: How ineffective is the company today, and how much room for improvement is there for generating more gross profit with the same number of employees? If we can get your RPE back to $110,000 per employee from the $80,000 today, we'll increase your profitability by $2.4 million."

Frank and Susan looked at each other, and the shock on their faces was obvious as they both shook their heads in disbelief. "Now that you put a number to it, I understand why RPE is so important," Frank said. "That's real money, even if some of our expenses go up."

"I'm excited—I think there's a great opportunity for us to make significant improvements over the near term," I said. "We determined that your company is operating in Quad 2, and we know that means both ROI and RPE are low—therefore, we can identify and implement initiatives and activities to improve both. The challenge we have is to identify your current levels of effectiveness and then identify those initiatives that will have the quickest and most significant impact on your organization."

I turned back to the whiteboard. "Organizational effectiveness can be measured by outputs from internal data and external data,"

I said. This time, I made two columns on the whiteboard, with "Internal Measurements" and "External Measurements" as column headers, and listed a number of items in each column.

Organizational Effectiveness

Internal Measurements

- Decrease in profit per EE
- Increase in expense per EE
- Decrease in revenue per EE
- Increased EE turnover
- Decreasing morale
- Increased overtime
- Increased errors or mistakes

External Measurements

- Decrease in sales
- Decrease in referrals
- Increased customer complaints
- Decreased customer satisfaction
- Decrease in client retention

EE = Employee

"Based on how I've written these, would they indicate an increase or decrease in organizational effectiveness?" I asked.

Susan quickly chimed in. "These would indicate a drop in effectiveness," she said. "If all of these were happening in a company, it seems like the company would be in serious trouble."

Turning to Frank, she continued, "Frank, I think if we measured all of these, we would find that many of them apply to us, except that our sales continue to grow." She looked back at the board. "Wow, I see a lot of areas where we can improve!"

"Alright, I buy into the logic that a 1 percent increase in effectiveness can improve profits by 10 percent and that Susan is probably right that we have a lot to improve on, but how do we do it?" Frank asked.

"Let's review some of the areas that cause these problems," I said. I added two columns on the whiteboard, listing out both operational and human capital items.

Drivers Behind Underperformance

Operational Infrastructure

- Accounting systems not designed to sustain growth
- IT systems falling behind trends and technology
- Limited financial resources/ financial resources consumed supporting growth
- Inadequate information for decision making
- Non-integrated systems
- Time spend on non-productive activities
  - Regulatory Compliance
  - HR Administration

Human Capital

- Finding quality employees
- Lack of clearly defined roles
- Managing and developing knowledge, skills and abilities
  - Lack of use of pre-employment tools
  - Inadequate training
- Lack of performance management systems
  - Clearly defined goals and objectives
  - Consistent and timely feedback
  - Lack of management development

"These are not all-inclusive, but rather a sample of the areas that contribute to lower effectiveness, both operationally and with people. For example, many companies have a difficult time staying up with trends in technology because of the rapid pace of change," I said. "Frank, tell me about your current IT infrastructure. Do you host your technology on premise? If so, tell me about it."

Frank nodded. "Yes, we do. We have a state-of-the-art equipment room that houses our servers. We had it built about ten years ago with all of the best technology. It's temperature controlled, and access is limited to our IT team and senior management."

"Sounds expensive," I said. Turning to Susan, "Any idea how much you spend a year maintaining it?"

Susan smiled and said, "I don't know offhand, but we have two IT professionals, and one of them spends a lot of his time maintaining the servers. Plus, we had one of the servers fail one time, so now we have a replacement plan to make sure we have current technology."

"You know your business better than I do, and maybe it gives you a competitive advantage in the marketplace to host your own server. But today, a new start-up engineering firm can spin up a server in the cloud in an hour and only pay for the space they're using," I said. "This may give them a competitive advantage over you, as they can either charge less per hour for their services, enjoy higher profits, or have more money available to pay higher salaries to attract high-quality employees. Thus, your IT systems may be very effective, but at what cost? Are there other ways to manage your IT effectively but at a lower cost?

"Let me give you a more comprehensive example," I said. "Susan, you currently manage HR for the company. How much time and money do you think you spend on HR administration per employee? Would it be $500, $1,000, maybe more?"

Susan seemed a little uncomfortable as she prepared to answer. "I'm not really sure how much we spend per employee," she said. "It probably takes 30 percent of my time, but as I mentioned earlier, I'm only doing what I can to keep up. I'm the controller and not really trained in HR. So I'm sure there are things we aren't doing that we should be. I'd guess we're probably spending no more than $500 per employee."

Susan's answer is fairly common among small to midsized businesses that try to limit the amount of money they spend on their HR infrastructure and support, which is often viewed as overhead that must be kept to a minimum. I have spoken with many business leaders who have not received a good return on their investment in HR, so they choose to get by with as little investment as possible. Small to midsized businesses are at a disadvantage, as it is difficult to acquire the necessary knowledge and skills across multiple HR disciplines within their budgets.

Yet, many studies have shown that companies that make strategic investments in their HR and workforce management outperform those that don't. The amount of investment varies significantly. A recent HR report indicated that the lowest percentile was $659 per employee, the median was over $1,600 per employee, and highest bracket was over $6,000 per employee (according the 2016 SHRM research).

"Susan, at that level, you're below national survey reports for the lowest percentile of investment in HR. That means either you're very efficient and effective at your management of HR or you're not doing some of the things you should be doing."

Susan was now very uncomfortable. So far, we had been talking about how Frank may need to change his decisions on how to run and grow the business. Now we were discussing the fact that Susan may not be doing all the things she should be doing to manage the HR functions, protect the company, and reduce risk. Also, the discussion highlighted that she has been inwardly focused and not thinking about how to meet the HR needs of the company today and in the future.

"Susan, I don't mean to put you on the spot," I said. "But I want to explain that as companies grow, their HR needs change and evolve." From my briefcase, I pulled out a few documents and gave them to Frank and Susan. "Let me explain."

HR Has Three Distinct Activities

"This triangle represents the three major areas of HR. The bottom of the triangle is the administrative HR activities. These are the treadmill of HR, the things that every company has to do every day—processing payroll, benefits administration, regulatory compliance and reporting," I explained. "The middle of the pyramid is the operational HR, representing those activities you do every day related to managing employees. Essentially, operational HR is about the employee life cycle—from recruiting to termination and everything in between. The top of the triangle, strategic HR, is where you make decisions on such things as compensation design, benefit programs, recruiting strategies, and incentive programs.

"Now on to the next page. I believe that as companies grow, the bottom line impact of HR becomes greater. The volume of the operational activities increase, the importance of operational HR expands, and strategic HR becomes critical," I said.

As Companies Grow, Their HR Needs Evolve

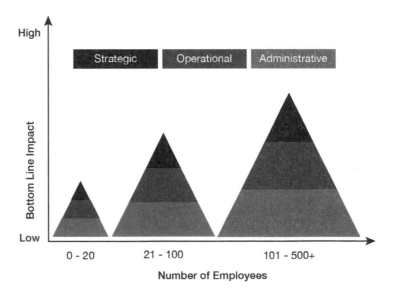

"However, most companies end up spending more and more of their time on the growing administrative activities that provide the lowest bottom line value. In fact, on the next page you'll see that there is an inverse relationship between the volume of activity and the bottom line impact.

HR Activities and Their Bottom Line

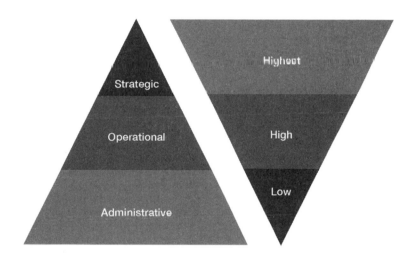

Impact is Inversely Related

"That which takes the most time and needs to be error-free brings the lowest bottom line value. You can't afford to miss enrolling an employee in benefits or missing a tax payment or deducting the correct benefit deduction from a paycheck," I explained. "Yet, the activity that is the highest value gets the least amount of attention, as the focus is on transactional and not strategic, and the middle section, perhaps the most important, needs never-ending attention from management to drive bottom line value."

> *Businesses need HR systems that scale with their company and meet their unique needs as they need it and when they need it.*

I didn't have to push down any further with my questioning, as it was obvious that the company had not evolved their HR practices along with the company's growth. Susan was continuing to play the role of the HR professional with practices unchanged from the company's early years, but the demand on the organization had grown exponentially. It was apparent to me that Frank assumed that by hiring more experienced professionals from larger firms, their knowledge and experience would just naturally transfer to his company.

Frank, now growing a little frustrated, said, "Are you suggesting that we need to hire an HR professional? Susan and I have spoken about it, and it seems that would solve a lot of the problems you've described. I guess we've just been trying to get by and keep the cost as low as possible."

"I'm not suggesting that you need to hire an HR professional or change how you run your IT systems, but I am trying to explain that we need to identify those areas in your business where we can improve both the operational infrastructure and human capital management to help you significantly improve your organizational effectiveness," I said.

Looking at Frank, I continued, "I've spent a lot of time with you and Susan to help us frame your current reality and discuss how you got where you are today, but we can't begin making changes in a vacuum. Our first step is to have an understanding of your plans for the future. We need to understand your business plan for the next one to three years and your key initiatives, and look around corners to anticipate the future. In other words, what will put you out of business? Think back to my Blockbuster story. They were in the Driving Zone, but then a disruptive technology quickly moved them into the Drama Zone and ultimately out of business.

"What are the threats to you and your business?" I asked. "What will put you out of business? Loss of a few major clients, a major employee lawsuit, or tragically you get hit by the infamous bus? Is your business prepared to continue without you?

"To get to Quad 4, we are going to do the following," I said as I began writing bullet points on the whiteboard. "First we are going to understand:

- Current and future challenges
  * Competitive environment
  * Business plan
  * Financial situation

"Once we have a good understanding of these items, we'll be prepared to do the next three steps. This will serve as your blueprint for the future.

- Operations—operational effectiveness
  * What initiatives will increase ROI
  * What initiatives will increase RPE
- People—HR effectiveness
  * How effective at managing costs
  * How effective at managing people
- Ongoing planning, monitoring, and adjusting
  * What needs to be measured
  * Develop your dashboard
  * Rinse and repeat

"Frank, can I take your business plan with me to review?" I asked. "I need a couple weeks to review and come back with my thoughts, observations, and questions."

Nodding his head yes, Frank jumped to his feet and was on his way out the door.

BLUEPRINT TO QUAD 4

Over the few weeks we had worked together, Frank and Susan had made good progress toward identifying the current state of their business. The journey of discovery is often the hardest to get started but is necessary to fully understand the current state of affairs of a business. In Frank and Susan's case, they didn't fully understand how to frame and think about the problems and challenges they were facing. At first, the problem seemed to be a poor morale issue. However, once we began to gather information and analyze results, an entirely broader issue emerged.

From a subjective perspective, Frank thought the company was doing well. Based on his gut feelings and the high growth they had enjoyed over a few years, the larger clients, and the growth of his management team, he placed it in the Driving Zone. He thought the morale issue was merely a nuisance that could be fixed quickly by bringing in an outside consultant to help identify a few issues and do a couple of training exercises, and that ultimately the morale issue would go away.

Susan, on the other hand, had a different view, which was both subjective and objective. In her role as both controller and HR manager, she had a front-row seat to the financial challenges they were facing as well as the employee issues that were arising. The challenge she faced was that her accounting and HR knowledge were having a hard time keeping up with the demands of a growing company. As the controller, she was responsible for managing the financial statements and reporting what happened in the past. As the HR manager, she primarily managed the administrative activities and compliance of the company. Now the company had become much more complex in both accounting and HR, and Susan knew intuitively that the business was in a Drama Zone.

It was apparent to me in the initial meeting that the issue was much more than merely a morale issue. In order for us to solve the problem, we needed to Go Slow and get to the heart of the issues. This required gathering historical financial data, personnel data, and operational assessments and analyzing the information.

Now we needed more comprehensive information about Frank's business to understand and lay out the plan for the future. In order to make plans and develop his dashboard, we had to have a clear understanding of where he was and where he is planning to go in the future. Then we will be prepared to identify those initiatives that will either control or decrease costs per employee and those that will increase effectiveness per employee (as measured by RPE)—and, most importantly, to identify what will keep Frank from going out of business.

WHAT WILL PUT YOU OUT OF BUSINESS?

I have asked hundreds of businesses and organizations this question as the starting point in planning for the future, and I always find it fascinating that a majority of leaders have never asked it of themselves. In fact, when the question is raised, blank stares are often the response. And yet, it is one of the most thought-provoking questions that a leader must ask himself.

It was September 29, 2008, that I posed this very question to eight business owners at an emergency summit I had called. On that evening, these very successful entrepreneurs were uncertain what the future held for their businesses. The economy was in a free fall, in the midst of what we now call the Great Recession, and that evening we didn't know how bad it would get. We knew that Bear Stearns had collapsed in March 2008, followed by the bankruptcy of Lehman Brothers in September, among other major government and institutional surprises over that same period. And then, on the 29th, the Dow Jones Industrial Average fell 778 points.

Up until this time, these individuals had enjoyed financial success, as reflected by their grown-up toys. The 29th was a kick to the stomach as their investment portfolios declined and the economy was on the verge of collapsing. It was at that point that we had to address the inevitable. What would put them out of business? To make matters worse, many of these entrepreneurs were in industries that were a part of the collapse.

The group of entrepreneurs included:

- A retail real estate investor
- A property management company
- A mortgage broker
- A dentist
- A residential subdivision developer
- A business services firm
- A large trade show supplier
- A charitable fundraiser

As we went around the table and discussed this question, it became apparent that everyone was at immediate risk. Some of the issues were easy to identify. For example, the retail real estate investor identified that his risk was his tenants and their ability to pay rent. It wasn't so obvious to the dentist, who felt immune to the highs and lows of the economy. The charitable fundraiser was already feeling it, as the donations were drying up more every day. As for the trade show supplier, he was adamant that he didn't have any risk, because his customers were the big automakers and they were immune to financial difficulty or bankruptcy. At the time, we all pressed him on his stance, and his opinion that he was immune to the recession was still fresh in my memory when GM filed for bankruptcy in June 2009.

Merely asking the question helped these individuals begin focusing on what they would need to do to manage through a recession. As the years unfolded after that evening, the entrepreneurs fought through many challenges to their businesses. Sales dropped, employees had to take pay cuts, customers went into bankruptcy, and banks reduced available credit lines. In other words, it was a perfect storm and challenge for these entrepreneurs to survive.

Fortunately, many years later most of the businesses survived and now are thriving. When challenged that evening to think about what would put them out of business, the entrepreneurs began to anticipate challenges, look around corners, and put together business plans to help guide them in the future.

The results:

- The retail real estate investor—Survived and thriving
- The property management company—Survived and thriving
- The mortgage broker—Survived and thriving
- The dentist—Bankruptcy from an investment in a commercial real estate transaction

- The residential subdivision developer—Bankruptcy as the bank called the notes
- The business services firm—Survived and thriving
- The large trade show supplier—Survived and thriving
- The charitable fundraiser—Survived and continuing to fight back

While there are many reasons that a business can fail, the following are some of the more common ones.

What Will Put You Out of Business?
Most Common Answers

Economy	Disruptive Technology	Lower cost Alternative	Failure to plan
Funding	Failure to Execute	Natural Disaster	Loss of key person

Disruptive technologies get the most ink for putting companies out of business or causing them to lose their edge. One of the most obvious now is the sharing economy. Uber and Airbnb are two of the most famous examples of the sharing economy and its impact on established business models. Uber completely turned the vehicle-for-hire industry on its head. A simple phone app and the opportunity for people to make a little money using their own car has decimated the heavily regulated and capital intensive taxi industry. Likewise, Airbnb has disrupted the hotel industry by allowing travelers to rent

out their homes and earn a little extra income from their proper-
ties—once again, technology allowing individuals to use their own
assets to earn money.

> *On a recent trip to Sydney, Australia, I used my
> Uber app on a Sunday morning to get a ride from
> our downtown hotel to a site twenty minutes
> away. The driver showed up in his shiny BMW
> and whisked us away. It turned out that he was
> an attorney on the way to the area where we were
> heading who thought he would make a little money
> and have some people to talk to on the drive. That
> is disruptive.*

I haven't sat in the boardroom of a taxi company or hotel
management company, but I would be surprised if the sharing
economy—which today is one of the fastest growing sectors of the
overall economy—was even on their radar a few years ago.

And yet, although not nearly as headline grabbing as disruptive technology, it is Failure to Plan that is at the top of the list of
these common answers, because during planning, ALL of the others
should be considered and addressed.

BUSINESS PLANNING

Preparing and updating a business plan is often one of the most
difficult endeavors for leaders and entrepreneurs. The daily activities
and pressures of running a business make it difficult for many leaders
to continuously review, update, and modify their plans based on
evolving business climates. In fact, when I ask audiences how many

have a written business plan, about two-thirds of the room will raise their hands. When I ask how many have updated it in the past three months, the hands drop to a mere handful.

> *NOTE: Business planning and strategy books fill the shelves of bookstores, libraries, and online stores and are beyond the scope of this book. From timeless Peter Drucker to contemporary Verne Harnish, there are substantial books that will provide readers with the thoughts, strategies, and business models to develop their own comprehensive business plans.*

With a business plan and supporting budget, a leader has the necessary information to establish targets for gross revenue and net profit. More importantly, if taken to the next level, the information is available to help businesses develop their dashboard to monitor ROI and RPE, and position their business to pursue Quad 4 success.

I have found that many leaders struggle to identify their key performance indicators (KPIs) as they look across their organization. With the vast amount of information they have at their fingertips today, the question is often what are the key indicators to monitor— or, in other words, what should be on their dashboard.

With their business plan and budget, business leaders have the foundational information required to build their primary dashboard that measures ROI and RPE, establish their targets for each, and provide the reference point from which to identify those initiatives that will help them hit or surpass their targets.

The overall process should include the following four major initiatives:

1. Planning and strategy—understanding the challenge (today, future)

- Competitive environment
  - What will put you out of business?
  - Identify external trends and disruptive technology
  - Technology
- Business plan
  - Strategic initiatives
  - Business goals (How fast will you grow?)
  - Where you are today
- Financial situation
  - Optimal ROI and RPE
  - Initial identification of dashboard items

2. Operations—assess operational effectiveness

- What initiatives will increase ROI?
  - Scalable systems
  - Outsourcing
  - Integration
- What initiatives will increase RPE?
  - Continuous process improvement
  - Reducing competency risk
  - Decreasing distractions from core business

3. People—assess effectiveness of personnel management (HR diagnostic tool)

- How effective at managing costs?
- How effective at managing people?

4.   Ongoing planning, monitoring, and adjusting

- Final dashboard

- Quad 4 measurements

- Continuously review and adjustment as necessary

FRANK'S FUTURE

I was thrilled when Frank returned with what appeared to be a comprehensive business plan. As I leafed through it, I was pleased to see that it had all of the major components.

Looking at both Frank and Susan, I gave them the following instruction: "Your job over the next few weeks is to pull together your management team and answer these questions:

1.   What will put us out of business?

2.   What will improve operational effectiveness?

3.   How do we improve the effectiveness of our people?"

With a big smile, Frank announced, "Our relentless pursuit of the Power of 10 to 1 begins today!"

Key Takeaways

○ What will put you out of business? At least annually, you and your management team should ask this question to help you look around corners and prepare for the unexpected. It is the one thing you are ultimately responsible for predicting so that you can make proper adjustments to your business plan.

○ What are the low-hanging fruits in your company — where can you make changes to your internal operations that will have an immediate impact on your company's effectiveness and improve it by 1 to 5 percent?

○ What are the key internal and external outputs that you need to measure to monitor your company's effectiveness?

○ What is the one thing you could outsource that will control costs, increase effectiveness, and give you and your company more time to focus on your core business?

CHAPTER 6

Shifting the Operations Gear

We were beginning to make progress, and I was thrilled that Frank and Susan were finally on the same page. It has been humbling for Frank to realize that all of his growth had actually put his company at risk. It was time to shift gears.

Frank and Susan had arrived to my office early for our appointment and were escorted to our conference room, where they were met with fresh fruit and refreshments. As I entered the room, I found the two of them enjoying their breakfast. Frank joked, "Wow, I'm going to start having all my meetings at your office. I could get used to this."

Before I could respond, Susan spoke up, "I couldn't help but notice the antique adding machine in the corner. Where did you get that? Does it work?"

I couldn't help but smile. "Yep, it still works. That Burroughs adding machine is over a century old and is from a small bank in southern Indiana. It was used to calculate all of the daily financial transactions. It is truly an engineering marvel, using gears and levers to add, calculate subtotals and totals. I'm sure the bank was thrilled to have this machine in the early 1900s, as it would have been much more accurate, efficient, and effective than manually tracking the day's activity. In fact, I love the advertisement from 1914 that I have hanging over it."

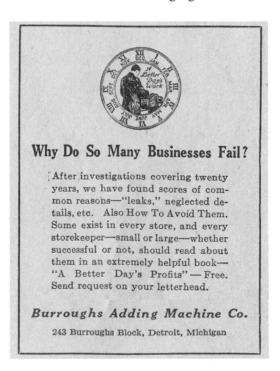

Frank went over to the wall and read the ad. "Wow, how prophetic," he said as he turned back around. "It's amazing that over a hundred years later we're still facing the same business issues. Neglected details."

I have had this antique Burroughs adding machine in my office going back to my days as a practicing CPA. It serves as a symbolic reminder to me to continuously improve efficiency and effectiveness so that businesses don't fail. It also reminds me that just because it works doesn't mean we should continue to use it. What antique technology, processes, or systems do you have in your business? What metaphorical gears do you need to shift?

"Frank, just like the gears in the adding machine that produce results, it's time we shift gears in your company," I said. "We're going to continue to be focused on efficiency and effectiveness." I placed my hands on Frank's business plan binder in front of me. "Your business plan is well done. I've reviewed tons of these, and yours is comprehensive and thoughtful. Fortunately, this gives us a huge headstart on our project."

Frank gave a slight smile and nodded his head in appreciation, but then let out a disappointed sigh. "Thanks for the compliment, but unfortunately my business plan didn't anticipate all of the challenges we're facing with our growth. Remember the employee who left to go back to his prior company? Well, he was working on a large project when he left. Unfortunately, his manager failed to transition this project quickly enough to another engineer and we missed a couple of big deadlines. Just yesterday we received notice that the client is terminating our contract."

I couldn't help myself but to have a flashback to our very first meeting when Frank described what he recalled as a major set back in his business when he lost his first large client after an employee left the company. It looked like history was repeating itself.

Pausing to allow Frank to get this off his chest, I asked the uncomfortable question: "How much will this hit your revenue?"

Frank was quick to respond. "Over $500,000," he said.

"Secondly, how much will this impact morale?" I asked.

"We haven't announced it to the staff yet. This is going to sting, and our business development team will be upset because this will hurt us in the market. The client is a well-known company, and they gave us a chance with this large contract," Frank explained. "Last time we met, you asked me to think about what would put me out of business. This question has been bouncing around my brain for the last couple of weeks. In fact, Susan and I started a list. One of the items was the loss of a major, influential client. Then that certified letter came yesterday. It was surreal."

Now I understood why Frank and Susan had called and asked to have the meeting at my office. As busy as Frank always seemed to be, I didn't think he would want to lose time driving across town to meet at my office. Now he had come face to face with one of those catastrophic type events. Fortunately, we had made some progress over the past few weeks and were prepared to move them forward. In an odd way, this event was making the issues real. No longer were we talking about hypothetical situations. We had a real event that had to be managed. It was loaded with issues—loss of revenue, management failure, morale concerns, impact on future business development, and reputational risk, among others. We needed to unpack what led to this, because if it happened to one, there may be others.

"Frank, I think we need to understand what led to this happening so quickly after your employee resigned. We need to understand if this is the only one or if you have other clients on the verge of giving you the same notice," I said.

Frank and Susan looked at each other in disbelief. It was obvious they hadn't thought about that possibility. Frank was first to speak. "Well, we have always had great customer service, hit deadlines, and produced a great product for our clients. I guess it is possible, but we've never experienced anything like this happening."

Susan chimed in. "How do we find this out?" she asked, clearly frustrated.

I got up from my chair and went to the board. "Let's use a common Six Sigma tool to unpack this problem," I said as I wrote out the 5 Whys diagram.

When working with businesses, I have always found it is important to press beyond the obvious problem or issue to understand the root cause. Asking "Why?" five times is an effective tool to get to the bottom of a situation. A friend of mine, a Six Sigma consultant, tells the story of how his wife bakes a ham, always cutting off two inches from each side of the ham before she puts it in the oven. One day, after years of watching her do this, he finally asked her why she cut off the two sides. She told him that is how her mother does it, so she does it that way also. After a long conversation, they decided to call her mom to find out why. Her mom answered that it was how she was taught to prepare the ham by her mom. Not satisfied with the answer, they finally called his wife's grandmother, who laughed and said, "My oven was so small that I had to cut two inches off each side before it would fit." Moral of the story: ask more questions.

I quizzed Frank and Susan about the reason for the employee's resignation. After fifteen minutes, I went up to the whiteboard and presented what I proposed was the answer to the questions.

I wrote in the answers to the 5 Whys:

Problem we are trying to solve: Client terminated contract

- Why—Missed deadline
- Why—Manager overwhelmed
- Why—Employee resigned
- Why—Manager difficult to work for
- Why—Wrong promotion or lack of professional development

From our conversation, it was apparent that the reason the client terminated the contract was missed deadlines. But when we pushed further, we recognized that the manager was overwhelmed, and that was because one of his employees resigned. Why did the employee resign? Susan gave the following explanation:

"From what I've heard, there are a few reasons he resigned," Susan said. "He told me he needed more structure, was working long hours, and just didn't feel like he fit in. Then when his former employer contacted him with a better opportunity to return, he couldn't pass it up. Also, there's a rumor that he didn't get along with his supervisor, which doesn't surprise me. Mike, his supervisor, has a strong personality and I've had a few of his direct reports in my office over the past few months with complaints. I've encouraged them to give Mike a chance, as he's new to his position and is still learning how to transition from a field engineer to a managerial position."

That gave me a good idea of what most likely led the employee to resign, triggering a series of events that ultimately resulted in a substantial client terminating their contract: Mike was not prepared to be a manager. It is often said that employees don't quit their companies, they quit their managers.

Frank finished off the rest of his coffee and sighed deeply. "I know what the problem is," he said, "but I'm not sure how to fix it. Mike joined me right out of college and worked his way up the ranks over the years; we just recently celebrated his ten-year anniversary with the company. As a result of our growth, we had a need for a new manager and offered the job to him. Mike is very demanding of himself, and I guess of others. Soon after we promoted him I realized that he's a better engineer working on projects than he is at managing people, but we just haven't had the time to work with him on it. Now it's come back to bite us."

"Frank, this issue is one of the oldest and most difficult challenges facing businesses today," I said. "When companies are growing fast, like you have in the past few years, it's extremely difficult to get it just right. The pressure of meeting the needs of the new business requires hiring and moving people into new positions and at the same time monitoring and measuring to ensure alignment with the company's goals and objectives. How do you free up the time necessary to allow you to focus on those critical initiatives when the demands on your time are never ending?"

> *Increased focus on core business is the first step toward increased effectiveness.*

Frank's business plan projected 20 percent growth each year for the next three years, and he planned to increase his staff from 80 to 110 employees over that same period. His assumptions for the growth were based on the company's recent success and growing reputation in the marketplace. This new information about the loss of a major client was going to challenge some of those assumptions. It is often difficult for leaders to take their foot off the accelerator on growth; however, if Frank doesn't get his foundation under control, the growth may be exactly what will put him out of business.

Opening the business plan in front of me to the summary page, I looked at Frank and Susan and said, "It seems we have a dilemma. Your success may be what puts you out of business if we don't get a handle on it. I'm sure you've already begun thinking about how the loss of this client will put more pressure on both your RPE and ROI. Also, the impact on morale could put more pressure on the organization, as employees will begin fearing the unknown and possibly be concerned about the health of the company."

Frank and Susan were both nodding their heads in agreement, and in unison said, "Exactly." Frank looked at Susan and then back at me and said, "That's exactly what we talked about on our way over here today. We both understand that the company is at more risk than we thought, and that we need to get our arms around it quickly. We're going to need an action plan when we share this with the staff."

"At our last meeting, we discussed the importance of understanding your current situation, business plan for the future, and financial situation," I said. "After reviewing all of your information, I think we're ready to begin focusing on the operational side of the business. We're going to focus on identifying those initiatives that will increase your RPE and ROI by increasing your organizational effectiveness.

"But first, we need a point of reference," I said. "We need to determine where your company is on the Quad 4 matrix today, compared to industry benchmark data and compared to your five-year trend. Previously we marked your company as follows, and now we'll add both 2010 and the industry benchmark for 2015:

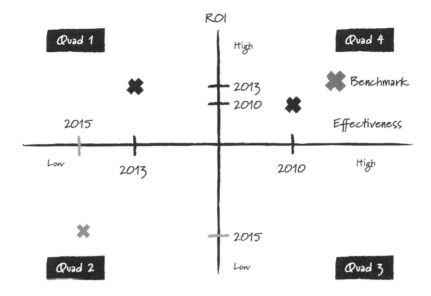

2010 ROI: 18%   2010 RPE: $110,000

2013 ROI: 20%   2013 RPE: $100,000

2015 ROI: 10%   2015 RPE: $80,000

Benchmark ROI: 30%[1] Benchmark RPE: $129,689[2]

"This gives us a good perspective of the path your company has taken into Quad 2. You'll recall how you were in Quad 4 in 2010 and then moved into Quad 1 in 2013 and Quad 2 this year. I've plotted the industry benchmark as the target in Quad 4.

"Because of your high growth plans, it would be very difficult for you to achieve the industry benchmark; however, we should set your goals for the next three years to achieve or exceed the industry benchmark to give the company a stretch goal. If you can increase

---

1   Figure for illustrative purposes only. Based on Deltek Clarity, "Architecture and Engineering Industry Study: 36th Annual Comprehensive Report, 2015."

2   "Architecture and Engineering Industry Study: 36th Annual Comprehensive Report, 2015," Deltek Clarity, accessed February 26, 2018, https://network.aia.org/HigherLogic/System/DownloadDocumentFile. ashx?DocumentFileKey=8a4dd73a-0941-4008-a9a6-f74b964cd170.

your RPE around 20 percent a year for the next three years, you'll outperform the industry. For your ROI target, let's pursue 10 percent total increases each year. If you can achieve both, you will be directly competing with your industry peers at the end of three years."

Frank sighed and said, "Wow, that really puts everything into perspective. I've heard it said that growth is expensive, and this really brings that to life. It looks like we have some important decisions to make if we're going to move ourselves back into Quad 4. I like the idea of setting three-year targets, and this will be very easy to communicate with the management team. It would be nice if we could get there more quickly."

"Agreed, it would be nice if you can get there more quickly," I said. "But again, your high projected growth rate will actually make achieving these goals even more difficult. As previously mentioned, we first need to focus on Going Slow, improving the effectiveness of both your operations and your people to achieve these goals. The first step is for us to identify initiatives that will increase your organizational effectiveness and also control costs to improve the ROI."

I moved to the end of the table where, in preparation for the meeting, I had already copied a chart onto the whiteboard that I planned to use to help assess the company's internal operating systems. "As you can see, I've already started a table for us to complete to begin this process. Across the top are criteria that I recommend we use to assess their importance and effectiveness. The most common internal systems are accounting, information technology, and HR," I said as I wrote them on the chart, "so let's start with them."

Systems	Integrated	Scaleable	Continuously Improved	Critical to Business	Market Differentiation
Accounting					
Information Technology					
Core HR					

"Susan, let's begin with accounting. To merely say 'accounting' is oversimplifying a complex system. As you know, accounting is not merely the generation of financial statements once a month. It is very comprehensive and includes setting budgets, managing cash flow, billing for services, vendor management, accounts payable, bank reconciliations, fraud avoidance, payroll processing, revenue collection, and the list goes on and on. Let's consider the criteria across the top with regard to accounting. The first: Is it integrated?"

It was apparent from the look on Susan's face that this was not going to be a topic she was excited to discuss in detail, as she took a deep breath and lowered her head. "No, the accounting systems are not integrated. For example, the engineering professionals manually track their time for each contract and submit them to my department once a week. My assistant then enters them into the billing software we use to generate the invoices for our clients. Unfortunately, the billing software isn't integrated with our accounting system, so we must make entries into our accounting system to book the revenue. This is only one example—there are others," she said.

I wrote "No" in the "Integrated" box. Turning to Susan, I made the assumptive comment, "If accounting isn't integrated, is it fair to say that as the systems are today, they aren't scalable in the future, aren't continuously being improved, are critical to the business, and don't give you a competitive advantage in the marketplace?" I filled in the remainder of the boxes and Susan nodded in agreement.

Systems	Integrated	Scaleable	Continuously Improved	Critical to Business	Market Differentiation
Accounting	No	No	No	**Yes**	No
Information Technology					
Core HR					

Before I could start the IT section, Susan said, "Let's go ahead and complete the HR section while we're at it. I'd like to finish the sections I'm responsible for."

"Alright, and similar to accounting, to merely say "HR" is oversimplifying a very complex operations system. Many people think of recruiting when they think of HR, but it actually includes at least thirteen subsections, including such things as hiring, firing, paperwork, government reporting, risk management, safety, policies, workers' compensation, employee benefits, performance management, and the list can go on and on," I said. "So, is it integrated?"

"No, similar to accounting, it isn't integrated. We use many different vendors, processes, and procedures to manage HR. I'd expect that there are things we should be doing that we aren't. It just takes so much time, and I don't have that much time to give to it. I just do what I have to do each day to get by. So, while you're at it, you can write in 'No' in the first three boxes. Also, similar to accounting, it is critical to the business, and I don't believe it differentiates us in the market," she said.

Systems	Integrated	Scaleable	Continuously Improved	Critical to Business	Market Differentiation
Accounting	No	No	No	**Yes**	No
Information Technology					
Core HR	No	No	No	**Yes**	No

It was obvious that Susan was discouraged by our conversation, as she turned to Frank and said to him, "I'm sorry that my areas aren't supporting the business as well as they could be. As you know, I put in long hours to keep everything moving, but maybe there are some better ways that I can help support the business."

"I wouldn't be discouraged with your answers," I said. "Remember, our goal is to find ways to improve your operational effectiveness. What we've uncovered is that in both accounting and HR we can make some changes that will have a big impact on the effectiveness of the operations. For this purpose, this isn't a discussion on individual abilities or performance but on the systems themselves." I turned to Frank. "Let's go ahead and complete this last section."

"I've already made some mental notes about IT as you've been talking," Frank said. "I think our IT is integrated, as our systems all connect with our servers; we have daily backups, firewall protection, and email on devices; and we use online services to store and access documents. Also, I think it is scalable and continuously improved, by the mere fact that the software companies continuously send updates. It is critical to our business but doesn't give us a competitive advantage in the marketplace."

Systems	Integrated	Scaleable	Continuously Improved	Critical to Business	Market Differentiation
Accounting	No	No	No	Yes	No
Information Technology	Yes	Yes	Yes	Yes	No
Core HR	No	No	No	Yes	No

"I think this gives us the information we need to begin making improvements in operational effectiveness," I said. "Based on how we completed this chart, it appears we have two areas where we can get the biggest lift and impact on improving the effectiveness. However, remember that the challenge is in improving effectiveness while simultaneously controlling costs. We can improve both accounting and HR, but how do we do it affordably? Finally, I want to challenge both of you on your assertion that these areas can't give you a competitive advantage in the marketplace, but we will address that later.

"Now we need to decide which initiative in these two areas will give us the quickest increase in RPE and ROI. Or, are there items that fall into both areas that will also have an immediate impact? For example, if we improve our accounting system, will we reduce costs and waste, capture lost billings, and increase cash flow? If we improve HR, will we be more efficient, get employees engaged more quickly, reduce risk, and free up time to be more focused on the business?"

I moved to the final open wall in the room. "Essentially, you have three options for addressing these items to improve these two operation systems," I said.

Option one: Do it yourself.

Option two: Partner with multiple providers.

Option three: Use an integrated managed service provider.

"Somehow I think you're going to show us that option three is the best," Frank said, smiling. "Since we began working together, I've learned that you're taking us on a journey of discovery and awareness."

OPERATIONAL EFFECTIVENESS

Unfortunately, Frank and Susan are not alone. I have found that many companies answer these questions in the same manner as they assess their basic internal operations, and often for the same reasons. Businesses are highly focused on delivering high-quality products and services to their customers; however, their internal operating systems often get the least amount of attention.

The goal of these underlying core business operations is to provide the business the critical support to meet its basic needs. If these are not efficient and effective, then they are a detraction—they waste valuable resources, increase risk, and take precious time away from focusing on the value proposition of the business. They become a major drain on RPE and ROI.

For Frank and Susan, the first step was to assess the operational effectiveness of the three core business operations. It isn't surprising to me that Frank assessed their IT infrastructure as meeting the needs of the organization. IT systems are often the one core operational function that get the most attention the quickest. When the internet goes down or the servers are offline, the business comes to a screeching halt and resources are quickly allocated to get everything back online and operational. Also, the technology industry continues to integrate their systems and software, allowing companies to access data, manage processes, and eliminate waste.

I recall many years ago when I carried a pager, a PalmPilot, a mobile phone, and a Daytimer to effectively manage my daily calendar, email, phone calls, and availability to the world. These were each great devices that made my daily business activities more effective. However, if I forgot to connect and sync my PalmPilot to my computer email program, I was lost until I could get back to my computer. Eventually, I added a GPS system in my car, and then ultimately had a Garmin that I could take with me anywhere I traveled. Then, along with millions of others, we moved to our beloved Blackberrys. What could have been any better? As we now all know, it didn't take long for Apple to turn the world on its head with the introduction of the iPhone. Today, technology has evolved and integrated to a point where all of the devices and so much more are reduced to a single mobile device.

Metaphorically, accounting and HR operations should aspire to be as integrated as the iPhone. The challenge is that both of these functions not only require technology but also require different levels of professional expertise that must be used in the right doses at the right times and in the right increments to maximize their effectiveness. Accounting professionals know that it takes a different skill set to manage accounts payable than to prepare a cash flow statement or utilize an IRS Sec. 704(b) real estate strategy.

Similarly, in human resources, the professional skills required for recruiting new employee candidates varies significantly from the skills required to answer employee benefit questions. The skills necessary for each of these is not something that can be easily managed by one individual and often requires subject matter expertise to manage them most effectively.

Competency risk is a risk that businesses face in many areas, but it is critical in accounting and HR. Professionals are educated and trained in their area, but both accounting and HR continue to grow in their complexity and demands, and it is difficult for an individual to become proficient in all facets. They are either destined to be generalists who have a general knowledge of lots of areas or specialists who have deep subject matter expertise. The challenge for many businesses is in how to get the level of expertise they need when they need it and as they need it.

Of the two functions, the accounting profession has the most established private and public accounting functions available to businesses today. Many professionals work directly in a private company and then use public CPA firms for specialized knowledge and skills. Today, CPA firms and consulting firms are offering CFO services on a part-time basis to fill in the gaps at businesses. By using these services, businesses are able to mitigate their competency risk at an affordable cost. I have seen many businesses with twenty employees hire a CFO only to find that they don't need the CFO's sophisticated knowledge, so it becomes an expensive hire that doesn't last long. They could have outsourced their entire accounting function and used a CFO on a part-time basis to monitor and provide guidance and advice.

The HR operational function is often the least-managed area within many small to midsized enterprises. Often it is viewed as more of an annoyance than one of a business's core operational functions. The activities are typically allocated to the person or area that is most trusted, or to the accounting department as a function of payroll. Frank's company is a perfect example of this, as Susan has been given the responsibility to manage the company's HR because she is the trusted employee who also manages payroll and finances. Yet, her professional skills are accounting related. Other times, businesses recognize the need for a dedicated HR professional; however, it is challenging to hire someone with the necessary skills affordably, given that the company is probably too small to hire the specialized knowledge they need.

Fortunately, the HR field has seen an emergence in both technology and professional firms to meet the needs of companies from start-up through high growth and maturity. The professional employer organization (PEO) industry is an example of one of those sectors that is providing the comprehensive outsourcing solution to small to midsized businesses. A PEO provides businesses a complete outsourcing solution for their HR needs by managing the core HR services of payroll, benefits and benefits administration, risk management, and regulatory compliance.

Companies have three options when looking to improve their operational effectiveness.

OPTIONS	ADVANTAGES	RISKS/THREATS
Do it yourself	• Full ownership • Determine destiny • Self-service	• Not integrated • Self-service • Unnecessary complexity • Lose focus on core business • Not scalable • Competency risk • Loss of key person
Multiple vendors	• Specialized technology • Subject matter expertise	• Not integrated • Service coordination • Unnecessary complexity • Lose focus on core business • Managing multiple providers • Not scalable
Outsourced managed solution	• Managed service platform • Scalable • Incremental professional support • Ongoing technology improvements • Transfer risks to provider • Mitigate/eliminate competency risk	• Selection of wrong provider • Perceived loss of control • Potentially more expensive initially

Most often, businesses find that using an outsourced managed solution provides substantially more advantages to their organization than does attempting to manage by themselves or with multiple providers.

It was Frank's opinion that his IT function scored high in each of the areas; however, there are areas of his IT that could be managed by professional firms that would provide immediate improvement and most likely help contain costs. The technology industry changes so rapidly that it will be difficult for his team to keep up with the external marketplace and take advantage of the specialized knowledge of professional firms.

MARKET DIFFERENTIATION

In analyzing business operating systems, it is critical to determine whether they can be leveraged to create an advantage in the marketplace. For example, a company may choose to use an IT firm to manage the servers and daily break/fix support while retaining their IT talent to focus on operational enhancements that reduce costs and increase customer service.

Similarly, a company may be able to outsource their HR to a PEO, which gives the company a new competitive advantage in the marketplace by offering higher quality employee benefits to attract and retain top talent. Also, by removing the non-revenue producing HR activity from the business operations and allowing the company to be more effective, the company has more time to focus on their core business.

Thus, one of the major drivers that need to be considered as companies analyze and consider alternative ways to run the business operating systems is to determine whether a market advantage can be created with their business.

PROCESS IMPROVEMENT

Toyota made Six Sigma Lean Process Management the pinnacle for continuously improving the manufacturing process. This approach has been adopted worldwide in manufacturing industries and is now making its way into the services industry. A book on improving operational effectiveness would be incomplete without recognizing the need for companies to adopt methodologies and systems that improve their operations and systems every day.

It is outside the scope of this book to delve into this vast area of ongoing process improvement, except to recognize its importance in the overall effort to improve both RPE and ROI.

For Frank and Susan, outsourcing their HR management to an outside firm could have the quickest and most direct impact on their overall operational effectiveness. Susan and Frank would have two immediate improvements in the organization. First, Susan would be freed up to spend more time on driving the initiatives that will increase RPE. Second, and more importantly, for the company to really drive operational and financial success, they need the HR infrastructure in place so that they can focus their energy on developing a high-performance workforce. But without the foundation, all other activities will struggle to gain traction.

Key Takeaways

O How does your company compare to the industry average? Are you outperforming on RPE and ROI? If not, are you close? What would it take for you to outperform on both?

O How do your internal operating systems score on the assessment? Are they scalable? Integrated? Mission critical? Provide differentiation in the marketplace?

O What other operational improvements can you make that will increase your overall operational effectiveness? Implementing lean process management?

O Implement the 5 Whys to problem solving and push for better answers than what often seems to be the obvious reason.

CHAPTER 7

Shifting the People Gear

The Burroughs adding machine in my office was superior technology in the early 1900s, but it was useless if someone wasn't trained on how to use the machine. Similarly, companies can have great technology and systems, but without a plan for developing their employees, they will put a ceiling on their ability to grow. Now it was time to shift the People gear.

We were getting hungry, and the three of us decided it would be good to get out of the office and take some time away from the project. We arrived at the local restaurant that I jokingly refer to as my office cafeteria because I eat there so frequently. It has a nice casual atmosphere, and most of the staff have been there forever. Many restaurants have trouble with high employee turnover, but not this place. As we walked in, the hostess nicely welcomed us, took us to our table, and told us that Cara would be our waitress. About that same time, Cara showed up at our table with water for each of us and some menus. Cara chuckled when she gave me my water and said, "This is two days in a row I get to serve you." After giving Frank and Susan their menus, she said to me, "You probably don't need this, do you?" We both laughed, and she told us she would be back in a few minutes to take our order.

Frank and Susan hadn't yet realized that there was a reason we went to lunch at this restaurant to talk about People. We could have easily stayed at my office and brought in food to eat and continued working on Frank's plan for getting back into the Driving Zone and pursuing Quad 4. But what we needed was to take a field trip. I needed to get both Frank and Susan to work *on* the business and not *in* the business. The best way to do that was to have them think about service from the perspective of the service industry. The restaurant industry provides a very clear example of overall personnel management. It is obvious when it is done well and when it isn't.

As promised, a few minutes later Cara returned and took our orders and refilled our water glasses. As she left our table, I turned to Frank and Susan and said, "They have great service here. Cara has probably worked here for at least fifteen years. In fact," as I pointed around the restaurant at other employees, "almost everyone here has been here a long time. One of the things I really like about this place is that they provide great service but also know when to give the right amount of distance if I am having a business conversation that needs a little bit of privacy.

"Their low employee turnover and quality of service is typically only found at high-end steakhouses and not a local pub. The owner really understands the importance of a good staff, and she works hard to support them," I said. "In fact, see the woman cleaning the table over there?" as I pointed to my right. "She's the owner. It's interesting to watch her run this place. She'll make her way around the room greeting guests, and then the next thing you know she is cleaning a table or delivering food. She sets a good example for what she expects from her team. They all work hard and are dedicated."

Susan had drunk about half of her water, and when she set her glass back down on the table it wasn't seconds before Cara arrived and filled it back up to the top. Susan smiled. "Looks like she isn't going to let me go thirsty," she said. "It can be so hard to find a good restaurant. I've found many places where the food is good but the service is horrible, or it's the other way around—everyone is really nice but the food isn't good. Why is it so hard to get them both right?"

"That's a great question," I said. "I think restaurants make for great business examples. In effect, they are a business model Petri dish."

Frank laughed. "I don't imagine the owner would like to hear you calling her restaurant a Petri dish! What do you mean?"

"Unlike almost all other businesses, restaurants provide their customers a complete experience in about an hour, and to be successful they need to get everything right. The moment you walk into a restaurant, you experience their branding, marketing, order taking, production, delivery, and ultimately the full service. If they don't get it right, the customers won't return and will probably tell others about their bad experience."

Frank chuckled and said, "You have that right. My wife can't help herself if she has a bad experience at a restaurant. She won't go back, and she makes sure everyone knows it wasn't good."

"When I go into a restaurant, I like to pay attention to all of the details to see if their business is in alignment," I said. "For example, I pay attention to the location, concept, decorations, food choices, prices, atmosphere, and of course the employees. Are they trained on service, the menu, how to talk to customers, etc.? I've been in many restaurants that have put a lot of time and thought into all of the details to create a great experience, but when the waiter arrives at the table, the experience is ruined.

"For example, recently my wife and I decided to try a new place that had converted an old Dairy Queen building into a fifties-style themed restaurant. We walked in around 8 p.m. and were met with a jukebox in the corner playing an Elvis Presley song, red formica table tops, and fifties paraphernalia everywhere," I said. "My initial reaction was that they had put a lot of thought into the experience, but then we were greeted by the waiter. The aggravated look on his face said it all, and he begrudgingly took us to an empty table. The experience went downhill from there, and to make matters worse we ordered milkshakes only to be told that on Mondays they shut down the milkshake machine early for cleaning. As you can imagine, we won't be going back. I really wanted that milkshake."

Frank and Susan both laughed at my story, and Frank said, "I haven't put that much thought into restaurants, but now that you explain it, it does make sense. In fact, it seems like whenever we don't like a restaurant it's usually because of the service."

"This is probably as good a time as any to talk about People," I said. "The second major initiative for increasing ROI and RPE is improving the effectiveness of your personnel management. I think restaurants give us great examples of both good and bad personnel management. In fact, it was in the restaurant industry that I first realized the importance of this issue. In high school, I was the night shift manager for a local pizza restaurant. Among many other things, my number one responsibility each night was to manage labor costs vs. sales. Every thirty minutes I would run the sales tape on the cash register, and then, based on volume, I would either keep the staff on hand or send them home. I had to meet the service needs of our customers but also control labor costs. It was a great lesson to learn early in my working career."

Frank smiled as he said, "I should have known that we weren't going out merely to have a casual lunch." Turning and looking at Susan, he said, "It looks like it's going to be a working lunch."

"Without my whiteboard, we'll have to use a napkin," I said, laughing. Pulling a pen from my pocket and grabbing a napkin from the table, I drew the Quad 4 matrix. "As a reminder, we need to focus on those initiatives that will control costs and those that will increase effectiveness. Let's talk about this from the perspective of the restaurant industry. We've already agreed that customer service is what will make a restaurant either succeed or fail. Let's make a list of those initiatives that will control costs and those that will increase effectiveness."

Susan reached down to grab her portfolio, opened to a blank piece of paper, and made two columns, saying, "I'll take a stab at this." She started writing items in each of the two columns. After a few quiet minutes of her thinking and writing, she turned the paper so that Frank and I could see it.

CONTROL COSTS	INCREASE EFFECTIVENESS
Reduce turnover	Reduce turnover
Avoid overtime	Hire the right people
Proper staff-to-sales ratio	Training
	Customer service
	Menu
	Motivation programs

"These are the few that I came up with off the top of my head," she said. "I put 'Reduce turnover' in both columns because if a restaurant can reduce turnover it will reduce their costs of training new people, and it will increase the effectiveness of their service. Just like your example of coming to this restaurant where the employees have been here for years."

I was impressed that Susan recognized that turnover was in both categories. In fact, turnover is not only expensive, it is one of the largest destroyers of organizational effectiveness. Turnover is actually the result of other problems. Some of these issues include not hiring the right employees, poor management, compensation, lack of proper training, and poor morale.

"I would agree with you on all of these," I said. "However, let's think about it another way. Instead of reducing turnover, what if we said it increased retention? Retention of employees is the positive result of our actions and activities. Also, retention brings us the highest return on our investment in our employees.

"Susan, as a finance person, you are probably familiar with the traditional break-even chart." I looked inquisitively at Frank, and he nodded that he was familiar with the concept. Using another napkin, I wrote out a simple break-even graph.

Break Even

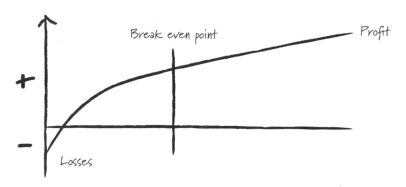

"A break-even graph simply shows that point at which revenue and expenses are the same," I said. "For example, let's say we purchased a commercial building for $100,000 that we planned on renting to a tenant. If the tenant paid us $20,000 a year, we'd break even in five years (5 × $20,000 = $100,000). The revenue we make after we hit the break-even point is profit, and we begin to get a return on our investment.

"I propose that the same holds true for employees. We incur a cost to hire and train employees, with the goal of getting them to breakeven as fast as we can to generate a return on our investment in them. If employees leave before we get to the break-even point or soon after, the business doesn't get the benefit of our investment in them," I explained. "Thus the goal should be the retention of employees; however, that is dependent on the business hiring the right employees. There is an old saying: Be slow to hire and quick to fire."

About that time, our lunch arrived. Cara, as if she were a professional juggler, carefully carried and served all three of our lunches, warning us that the plates might be hot and asking if we needed anything else. As if on cue, the owner of the restaurant appeared at her side with a water pitcher and quickly shared pleasantries with us. She thanked Susan and Frank for coming in for lunch and, as she refilled our glasses, asked them to let her know if there was anything she could do to make their experience better.

Because we were talking about customer service, it was obvious that Frank and Susan were more aware of the customer service and the environment. They seemed genuinely engaged with Cara and the owner. Frank was quick to thank Cara for her service as she offered him another napkin after noticing his lying on the floor next to his chair.

"It's the little things that make a big difference," Frank said, looking at me. "It's helpful to think about service from another perspective. We've been so busy working on my company that I haven't really thought about how I can learn from others."

My field trip seemed to be effective. Both Frank and Susan were now engaged and aware of their surroundings. Frank, who at times can be very intense, seemed relaxed and engaged, and Susan seemed to enjoy thinking about how to solve the problems of another industry. We enjoyed our lunch and took a brief pause from the intensity of the day. When we'd first met that morning, the stress of losing a major client was weighing heavily on both of them. As we talked about how to improve their organizational effectiveness, it seemed to give them some confidence about their next steps. Now we were beginning the next phase of improving their organization.

"Frank, my argument is that higher retention leads to higher organizational effectiveness, and the opposite must also be true: that higher turnover results in lower organizational effectiveness," I said. "The key point is that not all retention is good. In fact, if you retain low performers, they will have a negative impact on organizational effectiveness. The focus shouldn't be just on retention, but also on developing an overall process and methodology to develop high-performing employees and retain them and quickly identify those who aren't and make changes."

Cara had left our table, and the owner, whose name is Rosa, was in the process of clearing a few dishes from our meal. I looked up at her and said, "Rosa, I've been bragging about you and your company. What words of wisdom can you share with Frank and Susan on how you've been successful in building your staff?"

Rosa gave one of her famous warm smiles and cheerfully said, "It would be my pleasure, and I'm flattered that you'd ask. I simply hire for attitude. Good attitude is the foundation that I can use to help train a great staff. Bad attitude is a cancer and can spread quickly through our team. I learned many years ago that I could train on our menu and customer service but that it was hard to change attitude. Those with bad attitudes simply do not stay. That's my key.

The focus shouldn't be just on retention, but also on developing an overall process and methodology to develop high-performing employees and retain them

"We have a small company, so I handle all of the final hiring decisions. I make my stance on attitude very clear in the interview process, and our new hire training program reinforces it as well. We're quick to take action on someone with a bad attitude. A bad attitude will ruin a customer's experience, and as we all know, a customer who has a bad experience at a restaurant will tell five others about their bad experience. So when my staff comes to work, they have to leave any bad attitude at the door. The awesome part is that the team members will help each other if they notice one of their team struggling. They all pitch in to monitor and help each other. Thanks for asking, and let me know if there's anything else you need," Rosa said as she gathered the last dirty dish and quietly left our table.

Susan turned to Frank and said, "That seems a little harsh, but I can understand in a restaurant setting, where your employees are dealing directly with the customer, how important it is to have a positive attitude all the time. If we did that today, we'd lose twenty percent of our staff. I know that we have a lot of complaining going on, but I think it's mostly because of how busy we are."

"Susan, let's separate frustration from bad attitude," I said. "We know that morale is low and that there will be some negativity as a result. But do you have any employees who just have bad attitudes regardless of overall morale? If you do, they may be causing more problems than you're aware of and reducing the organization's effectiveness. Are either of you familiar with the Pay to Quit offer made famous by Zappos, the online shoe retailer?"

Both Frank and Susan shook their heads no.

"Zappos is one of the most successful online shoe retailers, which took the internet by storm and was purchased by Amazon in 2009," I said. "They understand the value of having dedicated employees who are committed to their standards of customer service. All new employees go through a four-week training program on the company culture, strategy, products, and customer service. At the end of the training, they are made a one-time offer—it was $1,000 at the start of the program—to quit the company. It has been documented that about 10 percent of the new hires take the offer. In fact, the company has continued to increase the amount, and Amazon adopted this same Pay to Quit offer at their company. Why would a company pay new employees to quit?"

Pushing my drawing of the break-even graph into the middle of the table, I continued, "The same reason that Rosa is quick to get rid of employees with bad attitudes at the restaurant; Zappos knew that getting rid of non-dedicated employees early would help the company move forward with only those who they can get to breakeven the fastest and would ultimately drive a high ROI on their staff.

"Have you noticed that this graph looks very similar to Quad 4? The vertical line represents ROI, and the horizontal line is effectiveness. Thus, another key to pursuing Quad 4 is to have a performance management system that helps you hire the right people, keep the right people, and retain the right people. I've broken these into five components of the employee life cycle, which I've defined as Find, Develop, Direct, Motivate, and Retain. The reality is that many companies don't have a comprehensive management system and only realize a small ROI per employee, but those that adopt management systems maximize their ROI per employee."

Implement Management Systems

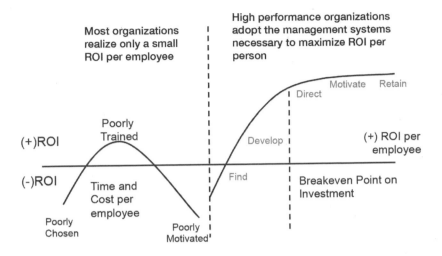

Implementing management systems that increase your ability to hire the best and retain the best will position your company to outperform the competition.

Companies that adopt management systems maximize their ROI per employee by optimizing practices across the employee life cycle—from finding employees to retaining them. Many companies, however, don't have a comprehensive management system and only realize a small ROI per employee.

As Cara cleared our dishes and refilled our glasses, Frank scoffed, "Well, to be candid, I haven't given much thought to our HR and personnel management. As an engineering firm, most of our employees are technically skilled, and their performance is measured by the quality of their work. We hire employees for their skills and expect them to meet deadlines. Also, most of our staff don't have client-facing roles. They work at their desks and communicate by phone and email. I understand that in a retail setting like a restaurant, customer service is critical to the success of the business. But how would a performance management system help my company?"

"No guarantee, but there's a good chance you wouldn't have received the termination letter in the mail this morning," I said. "If you had a management system in place, you'd be developing not only your employees but also your managers, rather than just assuming they know what they need to do. Remember, to get to Quad 4 performance we need to maximize our ROI and RPE. A good management system will do both."

After spending time with Frank and Susan, I would expect that they would complete my HR questionnaire differently now than when they originally completed it before our first meeting. I would expect that Susan was more accurate in her original answers than Frank, but she would most likely give them lower grades now. As for Frank, it was obvious that he didn't have a clear line of sight into his company's personnel management, but I am hopeful that he now has a better perspective and appreciates the importance of having an effective performance management system.

I was pleasantly surprised when Frank stood up from his chair and said, "Time to get back to work. You have me convinced, and I know where we need to start. We have a lot of work to do."

PERFORMANCE MANAGEMENT SYSTEM

People are a business's greatest investment and having an effective performance management system will have a signifi-

> *People are a business's greatest investment and having an effective performance management system will have a significant impact on the success of a business.*

cant impact on the success of a business. It is the ultimate key to building a high-performance company. The challenge for small to medium businesses is that the demands on the performance management system grow exponentially as the business grows. This is especially true in high-growth companies as their growth quickly outpaces the capability of the system, if there is one in place.

Businesses that Go Slow, taking the time to invest and build the infrastructure that meets their needs today and in the future, will best position themselves for success. The important elements of the performance management system include the five basic life cycle components.

Performance Management System

Find | Develop | Direct | Motivate | Retain

FINDING THE BEST TALENT

The first fundamental stepping stone in building a high-performance workforce is finding and sourcing talent. In today's workplace, the competition for talent is undeniable, and businesses of all sizes are competing for the best and brightest. Unfortunately, small to midsized businesses have historically been at a disadvantage when it comes to competing for top-tier talent against Fortune 500 type companies that have comprehensive employee benefits, extensive training programs, and long-term career growth opportunities. However, a shift is happening in the marketplace, as individuals are not looking for long-term careers as much as pursuing positions that give them the opportunity to use their skills in an environment that is rewarding and provides for personal improvement.

However, even with this demographic shift, businesses can put themselves at a competitive advantage by creating a comprehensive process for recruiting talent. Creating and following a programmatic process to recruit talent can be daunting, so many companies have turned to staffing firms and recruiters as their strategy for filling open positions. For small firms with limited resources, this may be a simple strategy that meets their immediate needs. However, depending on the position that is being filled, it may be an expensive option and may not deliver the necessary ROI.

Given the fact that high performers produce four times more than an average performer and drive significantly higher ROI, businesses that implement a comprehensive process are more likely to identify and acquire this top talent than those that are hoping to get lucky. This process includes such steps as identifying why the position is available; developing hiring specifications, detailed job descriptions, and talent requirements; and defining sourcing, screening, and interview strategies.

New technology and service providers are entering this space daily to help businesses meet their needs. In fact, there are almost three hundred different software companies promoting products designed to help businesses manage recruiting. This, combined with the extensive number of professional service firms that provide recruiting services today, is leveling the playing field. However, hiring top talent is only the first step. The big challenge is the rest of the employee life cycle, beginning with developing them.

DEVELOPING TOP TALENT

Sink or swim is often the mantra heard by employees as they join a new company. After the first week of introductory training and basic onboarding, employees are thrown into their new position. Upon coming into work the second week, they are met with the comment "Wow, you came back." While meant to be humorous, this comment should make managers and leaders question the quality of their performance management system. Successful businesses recognize that the investment to hire a new employee is only the first step towards developing an effective workforce. Once hired, the real work begins—developing employees to reach their full potential.

In Frank's company, as in many others, there was no formalized employee development program. During the first ten years of the business, the company grew slowly and new employees just learned on the job. In fact, many small to midsized companies use on-the-job training as their go-to development plan. This is a common practice for many small companies that are focused on merely surviving and for businesses that have modest growth and low turnover. Yet, this is a foundational cause of the Drama Zone for many companies as they outgrow this methodology. This is especially significant for high-growth companies and critical for their long-term success.

Starting with a structured orientation program designed to introduce the corporate culture, values, mission, and vision, the new employee is armed with the foundational guidelines for their future in the company. In the absence of clear guidelines, people will inherently fill in the gaps with their own assumptions or rely on prior experience to make decisions. This is why it is so important to have clear job descriptions written for each position. Employees need to have a clear understanding not only of the overall company goals and objectives but also of how their individual role in the company contributes to its overall success.

Many small to midsized businesses leave the responsibility for employee development to their managers. This manner of development relies on each manager's individual skill set and can vary widely across the organization, thus creating inconsistency across the organization and decreased effectiveness. A Quad 4 company will have both company-wide development programs and managers who are consistently trained on individual development.

An important part of a development program is the alignment of individual goals with corporate goals and objectives. This is often one of the most difficult and overlooked components of an effective program. It requires the business to have formalized corporate goals and objectives that cascade down the organization to formalize alignment. Otherwise, merely establishing goals and objectives in a vacuum or from the bottom up creates overall misalignment and decreased effectiveness.

DIRECTING PERFORMANCE

A highly effective workforce requires consistent and frequent direction and alignment. Not surprisingly, this is one of the most difficult areas of a company's overall performance management system to consistently manage. Yet, while it is difficult, it is absolutely critical to the overall success of a company. One underperforming individual can wreak havoc on a business, fellow employees, and customers.

In a very simple example, Rosa, the restaurant owner, sets specific expectations about what needs to be done, how it needs to be done, and the impact on others. She expects a positive attitude from all employees and makes it clear what will happen if they don't leave their bad attitude at the door when they come to work. She knows she can't tolerate bad behavior, as it would have an immediate impact on her business.

Thus, in order to be effective at directing performance, each individual must know what needs to be done, how it needs to be done, and the impact on others. By identifying these responsibilities of each job and choosing the right measurements, management can consistently direct performance. The key is to identify measurements that:

- Are hard measurements
- Are aligned with the company's goals
- Are under the individual's control
- Can be tracked
- That the individual has a clear line of sight to

One of the most common approaches for setting goals is SMART goals. SMART is an acronym for Specific, Measurable, Achievable, Relevant, and Time-bound. By choosing the right measurements, management has the foundation for giving effective direction and constructive feedback, documenting poor performance, and providing the opportunity for coaching.

MOTIVATING EXCELLENCE

A motivated, excellent workforce is the signature of a company in the Driving Zone. Oftentimes leaders confuse morale and motivation or use them interchangeably. The reality is that they are mutually reinforcing aspects of a highly effective organization.

Positive morale is very important in a company; however, it is hard to measure, hard to build, hard to define, and easy to lose. When discussing morale, it is important to recognize what it is not. It isn't appreciation, motivation, democracy, enthusiasm, or touchy-feely feelings. Positive morale is the feeling of well-being within an organization. It is created through clarity, consistency, and perceived fairness.

Positive Morale is Created Through:

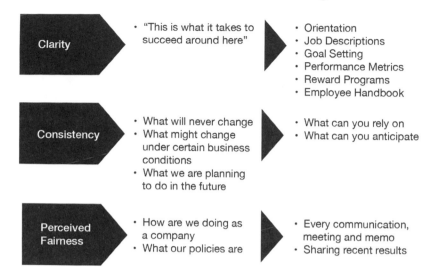

Clarity → • "This is what it takes to succeed around here" → • Orientation
• Job Descriptions
• Goal Setting
• Performance Metrics
• Reward Programs
• Employee Handbook

Consistency → • What will never change
• What might change under certain business conditions
• What we are planning to do in the future → • What can you rely on
• What can you anticipate

Perceived Fairness → • How are we doing as a company
• What our policies are → • Every communication, meeting and memo
• Sharing recent results

Positive morale is the foundation for a highly motivated workforce. Conversely, poor morale will undermine and inhibit motivation. Thus, highly effective companies understand why positive morale is critical to their success.

In Frank's company, poor morale is having a direct and immediate impact on the performance of the company. The company's lack of attention to building an overall performance management system has directly resulted in a drop in morale, which is undermining the success of the high growth.

Motivation programs are a powerful reinforcement tool to elevate companies to higher levels of effectiveness and performance. When built on top of positive morale, these work together to generate high RPE and maximize ROI, and are foundational components of a Quad 4 company.

Morale and Motivation

Reality: while morale and motivation are not the same, they are mutually reinforcing aspects of a high performance organization

RETAINING TOP TALENT

Finally, after creating a highly effective workforce, it is imperative to retain them. Outside recruiters actively contact employees, hoping to pry some away for opportunities where the grass may appear greener. Without a retention strategy, companies are exposed to promises of higher pay, less stress, more flexibility, and better career opportunities.

The cost of turnover is often estimated as high as 150 percent of annual salary. Frank's turnover increased to 13 percent in the past year, involving approximately thirteen employees. With an average wage of $52,000, the cost to Frank's business this past year could be over $1 million (13 × $52,000 × 1.5 = $1,014,000). We know that the contract lost as a result of turnover was almost $500,000 in revenue, validating the impact that turnover has on a company.

Companies must address the four types of turnover and establish plans to address each.

Kinds of Turnover

For purposes of effective management there are four kinds of turnover:

Correctable Turnover	• Poor Performers **Goal**: Speed These Up	• Good Performers Leaving • High Potentials Leaving **Goal**: Fix First
Unavoidable Turnover	• Job Transfers • Promotions **Goal**: Encourage These	• Retirement • Sickness • Death • Family Support • Reduction in Force **Goal**: Plan for these
	Desirable Turnover	*Undesirable Turnover*

All too often, firms retain poor performers and lose good performers

A concentrated effort on retention will pay significant dividends and drive up RPE and ROI. Also, companies must be quick to address the poor performers. A guiding principle should be to identify and develop the top 15 percent, retain the next 70 percent, and continuously upgrade the bottom 15 percent.

TALENT MANAGEMENT

Business leaders often refer to their employees as their most valuable asset, yet, like Frank, many have not invested the time and resources to develop comprehensive performance management systems. Without a plan of action, a business is only generating a small return on this significant investment and depriving themselves and their employees of the opportunity for optimal success.

Our lunch trip provided the opportunity for Frank and Susan to think about the importance of having a performance management system. Now, Frank knew what he didn't know. It was time for him to Go Slow to Grow Fast.

Key Takeaways

○ Is your company maximizing your return on investment from employees and getting them to a level of highly effective productivity quickly? Or are you only getting a small return on your overall investment?

○ Companies often don't know where to begin to implement a comprehensive performance management system. My recommendation is to identify the one area of the five stages of the employee life cycle that presents the quickest opportunity to have an immediate impact on your business and focus on it first. Then pick the next area, and so on.

○ Developing your front-line managers should be at the top of your list to focus on because they can have the quickest impact on overall performance.

○ Don't forget: employees quit their managers, not the company.

CHAPTER 8

Driving and Thriving

It was time to put it all together. Frank and Susan were almost ready to finish their first dashboard, and thus to begin moving toward a Quad 4 company. I knew the journey was only beginning, but I was excited for them to make the necessary course corrections for their future. It was time to raise the ceiling.

"I think I ate too much," Frank said jokingly as he took his seat in my conference room. "I could almost take a nap." As if on cue, a fresh pot of coffee was delivered to our meeting room. Frank hopped up from his chair and refilled each of our cups. "It starts with leadership," Frank said with a big smile, "and it starts now."

We all smiled and laughed with him.

With my freshly brewed coffee in hand, I stood up and went over to the whiteboard wall. "We've had a full day, so I think it would be good for us to review our time together over the past couple of months to make sure we're clear on where we are in the process toward helping you build a high-performance company.

"Initially, you contacted me because of a perceived morale issue in the company," I continued. I wrote "It started with morale" on the board, and then began to write each of the major concepts.

- It started with morale
- Lifeline—Performance and Time
- Driving or Drama
- Four stages of competence
- Quantitative measurements
    * Revenue per employee (RPE)
    * Return on investment (ROI)
- Quad 4 methodology
- Operational effectiveness
    * 10-1 vs. 1-1
- People effectiveness
    * Find
    * Develop
    * Direct
    * Motivate
    * Retain

After completing this, I moved over to another empty section of the whiteboard. I drew the initial Lifeline graph we used the first day

I began working with Frank and Susan—on which I asked them to plot themselves in either a Driving Zone or a Drama Zone.

"If you remember, the first day we met I asked both of you to plot yourselves on this line, and Frank, you put your X on the Driving Zone, and Susan, you picked the Drama Zone. Since then, we've spent a lot of time gathering the necessary information to determine that you were in fact in a Drama Zone. Also, I introduced you to the Quad 4 methodology and the key drivers of increasing organizational effectiveness as measured by revenue per employee and maximizing your return on investment.

"The key difference is that you initially guessed where you were on the Lifeline by your gut feeling. Then, as we introduced Quad 4 and looked at your results, we were able to quantify that you were in fact in Quad 2. Now let me show you how the Lifeline and Quad 4 work together." I added the Quad 4 box over the top of the Lifeline.

Performance and Time

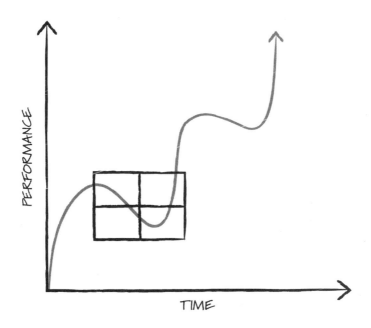

Before I could continue explaining how both of them worked together, Frank interrupted me. "I get it. How you plot your Lifeline is based on how you feel, and where you're actually plotted in Quad 4 is based on real data," he said. "Now I understand why we need to have the dashboard. By using a dashboard, we can set our goals and then measure how we're performing against them. Then we can make adjustments to how we run the company to minimize swings on the Lifeline curve. It all makes sense to me now."

Susan chimed in, "It makes sense to me also. I don't know why I didn't see it before. I can see how we were in Quad 4 a few years ago and then moved into Quad 1 and now into Quad 2. If we'd had a dashboard a few years ago, we would have been able to monitor the company's performance and make decisions more quickly to keep the company in Quad 4—in other words, in the Driving Zone."

Deep down, I felt a sense of relief that they were putting it all together. "You nailed it," I said to both of them. "Remember my example of the driver and the dashboard. An experienced driver is unconsciously competent using the dashboard instruments while driving. Similarly, if you have the right dashboard items, you can manage your company in the same manner. The goal should be to have the information that allows you to unconsciously and competently manage the business."

"Susan, why don't you come up to the board, and we'll begin to put together your dashboard," I said.

Susan shook her head as she said, "No, I don't have very good handwriting, and ..."

Before she could finish her sentence, Frank hopped out of his chair and said, "I'll do it. I need to stand up anyway."

Frank grabbed a marker from the tray, then turned to me and asked, "OK, where do I begin?"

"I'll start the dashboard, and then you can fill it in," I said as I drew a basic dashboard on the board.

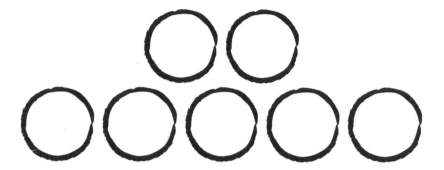

Frank went up to the board and said, "Based on everything we've talked about, it seems obvious that the top two critical numbers are ROI and RPE," as he wrote that in the top two circles. He turned to Susan and asked, "What else do you think we need to measure and monitor?"

Susan studied her notepad and leafed through the many notes she had taken during our meetings. "This is hard, but some of the things I've written down are growth rate, sales pipeline, client retention, employee turnover, morale, and customer satisfaction. There are so many things we can monitor, but I'm not sure which are the best. I don't want to pick the wrong ones."

"Don't get frustrated," I said. "All business leaders seem to struggle in identifying what the key things are to measure in their business. Let's start with your two primary items, revenue per employee and return on investment. What initiatives will you pursue as a company to increase both of these? Once we know what they are, we should be able to identify the key things to measure."

Now that Frank was up at the whiteboard, I sat down and let him be the scribe. "Frank, let's have two columns—one column

Operations and the other column People. Now we can list out the initiatives under each that you'll consider doing to help increase your organization's effectiveness," I said.

Frank turned to Susan and said, "These are some of the things we've talked about," as he wrote a list of items under each heading.

OPERATIONS

Integrated/scalable systems
Process improvements
Documenting operating procedures
Outsource non-core activities
Client retention

PEOPLE

Reducing turnover
Management training
Improving morale
Customer service training
Implement a performance
    management system
Hire top talent
Higher productivity
    per employee

"These are great initiatives," I said. "Now let's discuss which may have the quickest and highest impact on improving your organizational effectiveness and improving your revenue per employee. But first, there is another option that will immediately impact your two critical numbers. I know of an outsourced human resource provider that will provide you with an integrated, scalable HR system, bring immediate process improvements, decrease nonproductive time, provide a resource for developing your managers, assist in implementing a performance management system, and help hire top talent. This will give your company more time to focus on client retention and employee productivity. In addition, an outsourced provider will help you control costs, which drives your ROI.

"Now, of the initiatives in this list, what will also have a significant impact on the two critical numbers?" I asked.

Frank was the first to speak. "I think client retention is a significant initiative that will drive the critical numbers, and it's definitely something we should have on our dashboard. Also, we need to reduce turnover, as it has a significant impact on our productivity per person and should also help improve morale." Frank wrote these down on the dashboard. "Also, from Susan's list, I think we should add our growth rate and sales forecast. I've learned from working with you that our high growth is what got us in trouble, and we need to monitor our growth rate and future sales to make sure we're adding new staff at the right times."

"I think another thing we need to measure is the amount of time our employees are spending in professional development and organizational training," Susan said. "With our growth, the average tenure of employees has really dropped, and a lot of client issues tend to come from employees not knowing what and why we do what we do. So we need to measure the amount of time we're developing them."

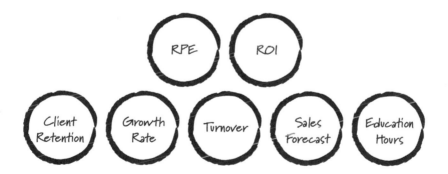

Frank sat back down in his seat, and the three of us studied the information we had gathered on the wall. "I think you've got a good start on your dashboard, and these are certainly measurable and meaningful items to measure," I said. "Your next assignment now is to develop targets for each of these so that you know what you're measuring against. Earlier we discussed your RPE target, and you have specific initiatives you've identified that will help you achieve those targets. In order for this dashboard to be meaningful, you'll need to establish an ongoing rhythm of updating and monitoring."

It had been a long day, and we had developed our first draft of the dashboard. Frank and Susan were just getting started on the journey toward building a high-performance company. We had come a long way from our first meeting, and they both had a better understanding of how the business had outgrown its capability to meet the needs of their growing business.

As we wrapped up the meeting, Frank used his phone to take pictures of the information we had on the walls. Then, as he gathered his notes and filled his bag with his materials, he said, "I expect that our staff will feel like they've been hit by a truck when I tell them about the client we lost today. But I feel much better because I know that I can also tell them I have a path to the future. I know this is only the beginning of turning the ship around, but now I know what I didn't know before."

"Frank, before you and Susan leave, I have a question," I said. "I noticed that you didn't put employee morale on your dashboard. Yet, that was the reason you originally reached out to me. Can you tell me why you didn't put it there?"

Frank smiled and said, "Originally, I thought you'd come in and do some team building exercises or other gimmicks to fix our morale problem. But over this journey I realized that the bad morale has been a direct result of my failure to effectively manage the company. I pushed so hard on growing the business that I assumed that my new management team would just instinctively know what they needed to do. I've learned that I can't just assume, and that we must have a programmatic plan to grow the operational capabilities to meet our future needs. Improving our team's morale will be a by-product of the work we're starting to do."

I couldn't help but give a big smile. I knew that our time together had been successful.

Susan began to speak but then paused and took a deep breath and said emotionally, "I want to thank you for working with us." As a tear rolled down her face, she continued, "I didn't tell you or Frank, but when we first started working together I was at a point where I didn't know if I could continue working for Frank and the company. I felt like I was failing, my morale was at a long-time low, I was working really long hours, and …" She paused and grabbed a tissue from the table in front of her. "But now I'm ready to tackle the future and I'm relieved to finally understand how we got where we are and excited knowing we have a path forward."

With that, our meeting came to an end. Susan and Frank both shook my hand as they left the room, and as we walked to the front door, Frank turned to me and said, "I think the first thing I need to do is talk to the HR company you mentioned. Send me their contact info."

HIGH-PERFORMANCE MANAGEMENT

Frank enjoyed success as his business grew from a start-up to eighty employees over fifteen years. Much of that can be attributed to his entrepreneurial instincts. Unfortunately, the company grew beyond his individual ability to effectively manage without a dashboard to monitor his key indicators about financial health and organizational capability. He was primarily measuring success based on top line growth and didn't anticipate that the high growth would add immense pressure on the company to execute.

An effective company dashboard is not static, but an ever-evolving tool for monitoring overall corporate goals and initiatives. Often I find that business leaders create business plans including such items as:

- Financial goals
  - Growth rate
  - Top line revenue
  - Profitability
- One to three-year initiatives to achieve the goals
  - New product lines
  - New markets
  - New distribution channels
- Workforce management
  - Compensation and benefits design
  - Hiring projections
  - Sourcing strategies
- Operations and infrastructure
  - Technology upgrades
  - System improvements
  - Cost management

Leaders then choose financial results to monitor because they are easiest to measure and report. Go to any investor website about the stock market, and headlines focus on revenue growth and earnings reports. Or at a cocktail party, when asked how a company is doing, many respond easily with information about growth and profits. The reality is that these only tell part of the story. Yet, most business leaders rely on just these measurements to monitor their company and whether it is on target to meet their goals.

OPERATIONAL DASHBOARD

The much more difficult but extremely important measurements are those that measure the organization's effectiveness. Building an operational dashboard requires both financial and nonfinancial data. As discussed, the RPE and ROI are the two critical numbers to monitor, as they provide information on how effective and efficient the company is operating as a result of their large investment in their workforce.

The other measurements are based on both external and internal outputs. These measurements provide critical information to monitor to help management make timely adjustments and course corrections. The key is to identify all that could be measured and then, based on the company's corporate initiatives, select those that are the most important.

Frank's company was a good example of the complexities that businesses face when they experience high growth. During our time together we identified:

- Drop in morale
- Increasing turnover
- Decreasing revenue per employee
- Decreasing return on investment from employees
- Drop in client retention
- Decrease in average tenure of employees
- Loss of a major client
- Operational weaknesses
- Weak performance management practices

These were all blindspots to Frank, as he was focused on top line growth and the outside success he was enjoying. Susan, on the other hand, was experiencing many of these but didn't know what to do. After gathering the information and assessing their organization, they were able to identify the Quad in which they were operating and could compare to industry benchmarks and historical data. Then they chose those initiatives to move the business toward Quad 4 performance. After they chose their initiatives, they were able to choose the items to put on their operational dashboard.

ONGOING PLANNING, MONITORING, AND ADJUSTING

Leaders who Go Slow and invest the time to strategically think and execute are better positioned to manage their company's Lifeline and Grow Fast, minimizing the fluctuations that occur when a business outgrows its underlying business capabilities, and to help anticipate disruptors that will greatly impact the existing business model.

Leaders who Go Slow and invest the time to strategically think and execute are better positioned to manage their company's Lifeline and Grow Fast.

Various strategic planning tools and coaching groups exist today to help business leaders establish a comprehensive and effective strategic plan for their organization. These tools and groups provide the thought leadership and environment to facilitate the planning process. As a part of the planning process, leaders must identify those key numbers that need to be measured to monitor the overall effectiveness of the organization.

Revenue per employee is the ultimate measure of organizational effectiveness and is a by-product of all other activities. However, it must also be measured against the return on the investment to generate the revenue. These two critical numbers are the scorecard for success. In other words, these give the results but not the "how." The "how" is the strategy and execution of the initiatives that were chosen.

The first step is to establish the target RPE for a business. This will vary by industry, so it is important to gather industry data to measure against. The software industry, for example, will have a substantially higher RPE than a law firm, because once the software is created, the revenue isn't limited by the number of internal employees but is highly scalable. On the other hand, a law firm generates revenue from billable hours; thus, the law firm revenue is highly dependent on the number of employees and their overall personal effectiveness.

Benchmark data from the same or similar industries is a great place to start when identifying the target RPE, providing a reference for how other competitors of similar size perform. Not all industries have competitor information available, so leaders may need to be more expansive in their research to identify similar types of businesses with which to compare.

Once the target is established, the next step is selecting the initiatives to meet targeted RPE and ROI goals. In the case of Frank and Susan, they found after assessing the organization that there were many different challenges impacting RPE. The high growth resulted in hiring many new employees, which in turn decreased overall employee tenure and the firm's institutional knowledge. Then morale began to drop along with client retention. Frank and Susan had begun to put together the initiatives that would begin to turn the company back around.

However, what if Frank and Susan had begun with establishing a target RPE before they began pursuing the high growth? They would have considered the impact the growth would have on their company and hopefully would have identified those areas that would need to be strengthened or improved to support the growth.

Now, with a clear understanding of where the business is positioned on the Quad 4 matrix and a comprehensive assessment of the operational effectiveness, management is prepared to identify and implement the initiatives to pursue Quad 4 performance.

After choosing the dashboard items, it is important to identify the correct timing and rhythm for monitoring. This will depend on the type of business, the items chosen, the growth velocity of the business, business cycles, and critical nature of the items.

Finally—and most important—is the need to continuously review the current progress, identify new initiatives, and plan for the future to keep the company in Quad 4.

Key Takeaways

○ Are you in the Driving Zone or Drama Zone? What Quad are you in? Are you able to unconsciously and competently manage your business? These are questions that need to be asked and answered as you begin your journey of becoming a Quad 4 company.

○ What are the key initiatives that will increase your effectiveness?

○ What will you put on your dashboard?

○ The faster you grow your company, the more pressure will be put on the management team to get it right. The world is littered with companies that didn't Go Slow—didn't anticipate the future, didn't control their growth, and didn't develop their organizational effectiveness to meet the future challenges and opportunities.

○ Ultimately it is management's responsibility to anticipate the future, minimize Drama Zones, and strive to be a Quad 4 company.

EPILOGUE

It was Saturday on a cool autumn morning, when I sat down at my home office computer to check on the news and catch up on emails, that I noticed an email from Frank. I was slightly concerned, given that he sent it at 10:38 p.m. on Friday, and opened it immediately.

Subject line: Morale

Hi Brent,

I hope you are doing well and wanted to give you a quick update on how we've progressed over the past three months. I've just arrived home from a dinner event with my management team where we celebrated our successes of the past quarter. After we left your office a few months ago, I was determined to get the ship turned around, and you will be thrilled to know that we have made solid strides.

First, I didn't realize until our meeting in your office that Susan was ready to quit. I am so thankful that our time together gave us the insight to understand where we were and to lay out a plan for the future. Candidly, I just didn't know what I didn't know. Today, Susan is excelling above and beyond what I thought she could do. She has embraced the dashboard and reporting and gives the management team weekly updates on our key numbers.

One of the first things we did was to outsource our HR. It was a little rocky at first, as we had to learn and adapt to new ways of doing things. It's hard to change from how you have done things for fifteen years. But we have made great progress, and we are now able to focus on the business of our business. Also, they helped us fix some major compliance issues that could have been financially ugly for us.

Next, we were able to save that major client who terminated their contract. When we looked at the impact the loss was going to have on our numbers, we knew we had to fight to keep them, and once we explained our dashboard to the management team, we all quickly agreed that would be our first step. It wasn't easy, but we met with their management team and explained what had led to our problems. We learned that they wanted to work with us but didn't think we'd be able to meet their needs. After hearing of the steps we were putting in place to improve our organization and meet their needs, they agreed to a probationary period. That is all we could ask for, but we are thrilled to have the opportunity.

Finally, I am writing this to you late on Friday night to thank you for providing me with the insight and direction to build a Quad 4 company.

By the way, our morale hasn't been this good in years.

Sincerely,

Frank

The End.

ACKNOWLEDGMENTS

First, I want to thank Bill O'Connell who assisted me as we explored and identified the underlying conflicts entrepreneurs face as they grow their businesses. Bill challenged me to look beyond the obvious and to think in multiple dimensions. Our work together was foundational for the content of this book.

Of course, I would like to thank the many entrepreneurs, clients, and colleagues over the past twenty-five years who allowed me into their personal worlds to understand the businesses, goals, and struggles that they face each and every day. Their candor and openness provided me with years of information and context to help analyze, guide, and develop the tools to help businesses grow and prosper. Specifically, I want to thank Brady Clements, Derrick Christy, Scott Smith, Jim Landwerlen, Peter Broscoe, Brian Wright, Tim Pierce, Mike Heffner, Tony Alderson, Chad Collier, Matt Claymon, Rob Glass, Steve Booher, Jeff Hagerman, John Norton,

Mike Link, Brian Mann, and Steve Peabody. Your friendship and business acumen have all contributed to my ongoing pursuit.

I want to thank my team at Tilson HR who have been with me on this journey over the years and have contributed their time and effort to the ongoing development of our programs and services. A special thanks to my assistant, Debbie Wood, who somehow managed to coordinate my schedule to find the time to write this book.

Thanks to my father and business partner, Jack Tilson, who has put his trust in me and has given me the confidence to reach higher and further than I could have ever dreamed. Of course, many thanks to my mom, Patricia Tilson, whose words of encouragement and gentle smile have always been my rock.

Thanks to my wife, Bridget, for her unrelenting commitment to a loving household and for raising our four beautiful daughters while carrying the burden of an entrepreneur's wife and also pursuing her equestrian dream with her horse, Buddy.

I want to thank my daughters, Becky, Brooke, Blair, and Brielle, for their unconditional love and support. I am very proud of each of you every day as you have grown into wonderful women. Becky, you have taught me to pursue destinations unknown. Brooke, you have given me the joy of generations. Blair, you have challenged me to live outside my comfort zone. Brielle, you have humbled me with the pursuit of knowledge and the unknown.

Thanks to my colleagues in the Professional Employer Organization as we have built the industry through hard work, dedication, and commitment. We focus on providing services that are the backbone of the entrepreneurial community and help companies grow faster and be more successful.

A big thanks to Verne Harnish who challenged me to own my ink and my Gazelle's coach, Dr. Craig Overmyer, for his ongoing commitment to making this a great book. Craig invested numerous hours reviewing my content, making critical observations, and encouraging me to find my voice.

I must also thank the late Dr. William Haeberle, Professor Emeritus, Indiana University Kelley School of Business, whose entrepreneurial wisdom, spirit, instruction, and encouragement were instrumental in my professional growth. He was a great friend and mentor.

Thanks to those who have supported me throughout the writing of this book by reading from the early manuscripts through the final edits. Their valuable feedback and encouragement helped me push through to the end. First, I want to thank my daughter, Blair Mulzer, for her detailed review and edits. Next, I want to specifically thank Jessi Robbins, Debbie Wood, Pat Cleary, Phil Powell, Jason Mizen, Aaron Prickel, Will Ditzler, Chad Collier, Steve Palamara, Rob Glass, Chris Reed, and Deana Haworth who gave their time and talents to make this a better book.

I must thank the team at Advantage|ForbesBooks for their ongoing help and support in writing this book. My writing coach, Josh Houston, has been there with me throughout this project to encourage, challenge, and guide me. His ability to provide broad perspectives, yet also dive deep into the content, has been critical to the success of the book.

Finally, I am thankful to be covered by the grace of my Lord Jesus Christ; without Him I am nothing.

A Special Offer from ForbesBooks

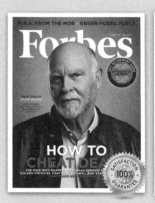

Other publications bring you business news. Subscribing to *Forbes* magazine brings you business knowledge and inspiration you can use to make your mark.

- Insights into important business, financial and social trends
- Profiles of companies and people transforming the business world
- Analysis of game-changing sectors like energy, technology and health care
- Strategies of high-performing entrepreneurs

Your future is in our pages.

To see your discount and subscribe go to Forbesmagazine.com/bookoffer.

Forbes